Johnny be good

Johnny be good
out from the darkness: an incredible true story

Johnny Kinch

appleyard PRESS

Loughborough
2008

appleyard PRESS

Appleyard Press
Loughborough
Leicestershire
LE11 3QJ, UK

© Kinch, J. (2008)

Kinch, J. (2008)
Johnny be good
Out from the darkness: an incredible true story
Appleyard Press, Loughborough, Leicestershire, UK

ISBN paperback 978 0 9558659 0 9

Printed by J. H. Haynes & Co. Ltd., Sparkford

Designed and produced by Appleyard Press

Acknowledgements

First and foremost I would like to thank Anneka, my best friend and wife. She has had to put up with my constant waffling as I wrote then re-wrote this book. She is an absolute inspiration to me and I thank God everyday for blessing me with such a beautiful and sincere woman. If it wasn't for Jesus we would never have met. She has led a life that is so contrary to mine that anyone in their right mind wouldn't put us together. But thankfully God knows best!

Then there's my mate Simon Smith, what can I say. He not only helped me out financially making this book possible, but also gave me invaluable advice after reading the first draft, that helped make my story readable. Thanks pal!

Also I'd like to thank Pablo Raybould, who spent countless hours proof reading and making the text flow like a river (no small task) and Sue Plummer who designed the cover and typeset the book, amongst a thousand and one other things. I would like to add that all the above, gave their time and expertise free of charge for which I will be forever indebted.

Thanks to my good mate Swanny for his continuing support. To my Mum who was there when I needed her. To Pastor Barry Thomas and his lovely wife Josephine and all at Without Walls Christian Fellowship in Stanton Under Bardon. And finally, my good friend Jonnie Cave. If it wasn't for his obedience to God, a life of love, joy and fullfilment would never have been mine. Thank you brother!

Johnny Kinch

WARNING!
You may find some parts of this book grammatically incorrect and not in chronological order. Get over it!

This book was written with the intention of being used as an evangelistic tool, to win hearts and minds for Christ.

The majority of names have been changed to protect the individuals mentioned.

For Anneka ...

Contents

1

Super hero

I'm completely out for the count. No sound, no light, no feelings, just darkness. I'm awoken by the sound of a taxi horn. My mouth is dry and tastes like crap and somehow I manage to open my eyes. I'm living on the streets and in the gutter again. It's still dark and my watch tells me its 4.20 am. I'm drawn to something moving behind me. I turn over and lying next to me is an old, grey haired, thin man with his trousers round his ankles. As my eyes clear I see a belt round his leg like a tourniquet and a needle sticking out of his bony knee. I'm not shocked by what I see but I jump up quickly and start checking myself over to make sure I'm ok. After so much alcohol the night before, sudden movements are not a good idea. My head is pounding and I nearly faint on the spot. I manage to steady myself and take stock of the situation then I'm brought back to reality and remember why I'm here.

Looking up through a break in the clouds I can see the stars. For a moment I feel hope and remember what Oscar Wilde once said, "We are all in the gutter but some of us are staring at the stars." That summed me up. People used to say that I could fall into a bucket of s**t and come out smelling of roses. I even started to believe it myself. Little did I know where this next journey would take me and to what extent I'd fall.

I was outside a hostel called St. Mungo's at 83 Endell Street in Covent Garden. I'd been homeless this time for about three weeks and had been told by a fellow homeless guy nicknamed 'Geordie', for obvious reasons, that St. Mungo's took in self referrals. Meaning, anyone could refer themselves from the street for a room without going through the social first. I had been to see the staff there the night before and was told that they open at 7.00 am and to come back then. I got there hoping, on the off chance, there was a vacancy but I was way too early. I had been busking the day before and had a couple of quid on me for emergencies. When I busked, I didn't use an instrument of sorts but I knew quite a lot of Shakespeare from my RADA days (Royal Academy of Dramatic Art) and would entertain people in beer gardens with the odd sonnet or two for beer money.

I felt really rough. I wasn't going to hang around the hostel until it opened so I headed off towards the only offie I knew that would sell me booze at that time of the morning.

Thank God it was open. This particular offie was well known amongst the alcoholic fraternity and you could get a drink there ninety nine times out of a hundred no matter what the time was. After a bit of banter with the shop keeper 'Effie', I cracked open a can of Tenants Extra and began to pour it down my throat. I needed some blood in my alcohol stream; I used to say to people as a joke. As the booze went into my system I started feeling a bit drunk again and the pain of sleeping on the streets and the chill from the cold night air began to melt away. I wandered around until I found a bench near the Hostel and sat there drinking, wondering where it had all gone wrong.

My name is Jonathan Paul Kinch or Johnny to those who know me. I was born in March 1971 on the kitchen table of 205 Aylestone Road in Leicester. I still have the splinters in my bum to prove it! I'm only joking.

I lived there for a year then moved to Woodhouse Eaves with my Mum, Dad and Jason, my only brother at the time. Woodhouse Eaves is a lovely, picturesque village on the outskirts of Loughborough in Leicestershire.

I went to the local school of St. Paul's and had quite an ordinary couple of years there. The only incident worth noting happened on my 6th birthday. I had been given some kind of super hero suit as a present. When I wore it I'd get lost in my own imagination (which was easy for me). My older brother Jason was much smarter than me at the time and must have seen how wrapped up I could get. We were quite close in years and used to argue a lot, always looking for ways to get at each other. This must have seemed like a golden opportunity for him and late in the morning I found myself upstairs being talked into jumping from our bedroom window, told that I could fly. Well it made sense to me, after all, I had the suit and, as it didn't look that far down, I threw caution to the wind and out I went.

As my feet hit the concrete two floors down my knee was thrust upwards towards my open mouth. As my knee hit my jaw I bit down so hard on my tongue that I almost bit it in half. Bent double, my body took the full impact of the fall and I fell forward damaging my back as a result. Immediately the blood started to spurt from my mouth and a worried, wide-eyed Jason appeared on the scene. As soon as he saw all the blood coming out my mouth he ran off to alert my mother in the kitchen.

The next thing I can remember is being carried into the ambulance on a stretcher and the last image I saw was Jason sticking his tongue out at me as I was whisked off to the hospital.

My father was working away when he got the news of my accident. I think he was on a building site somewhere. He was a really strong bloke, about six feet tall, short dark hair and good looking with it too, a proper man's man. As soon as he got the message about his little boy he left his job and thumbed a lift to the hospital to see me. He had been told that I had internal bleeding and was in a bad way.

Thankfully my injuries weren't as bad as first thought and I was let out pretty soon and sent home with a badly bitten tongue and a very sore back.

Looking back I was lucky that I didn't lose my tongue that day. A lot of trouble would have been avoided if I had bitten it off completely as it was my gob that got me into so much bother in the past, as you will see. Thankfully it's used mostly for good now.

2
Stump

Bzzzzzz, click. Staff unlock the magnetic door to the hostel and let me in. I go to the reception desk and tell the young lady who I am. She seems nice and not as stuck up as the others I've met. Her name is Claire; she has thick brown hair tied back and is dressed like someone you would see at Glastonbury. "Come this way" she says and takes me down a long corridor into a back room where I'm told to sit and wait while she fetches the paperwork. It's a really old eight-storey building, all the walls are painted lime green and the whole place smells like an old peoples home. It used to be a school, except you would never have known that young people once had fun there and it now felt more like an open prison. I let out a sigh as I tried to relax in the chair. I'd got to get into this one. I couldn't cock this up. I was so tired, my body was aching all over and my brain felt like it could shut down at any minute. Another staff member came in, this time a small Irish fellow with a bald head and a chip on his shoulder.

"Name?" he asked abruptly.

"Johnny Kinch," I replied.

"Age?"

"28."

"Do you have a drink problem?"

"No," I said.

"How about drugs?"

"Definitely not!" I said (all lies). And on and on the questioning went for about an hour until we had completed all of the relevant paperwork. I tried to paint a good picture of myself and made it sound so good that even I believed most of it. I think that's what made me so convincing. He left the room to talk with colleagues and I tried to make myself look

5

as dishevelled as possible, which didn't take much as I had been sleeping rough and was good at laying it on with a trowel (exaggerating).

The door opened and I looked up to see Claire smiling down at me. "We have a vacancy and the room is yours," she said. I was so relieved to hear those words but too exhausted to show it.

I was taken upstairs to the second floor and shown into room number 205. The room was dark and dingy; it had two single beds, two small wardrobes and a sink. The beds were made of metal frames with zigzag springs, the kind you would see in documentaries about the 1st World War. On top of each bed was a green, plastic coated mattress. They were plastic coated so they were easier to clean when residents crapped or wet the bed. As the door closed I collapsed onto my bed under one of the standard issue blankets and fell asleep.

I felt much stronger after my sleep and woke up facing the wall. I was so tired, before I'd dropped off, that I hadn't even noticed the graffiti all over it, left there by former residents. The room was much darker now; I must have been out for hours. I could hear traffic and the hustle and bustle of Covent Garden as people made their way out of the city. Then, as I started to fully awake my ears picked up on an altogether different sound. There was someone breathing heavily and it was coming from inside the room. I slowly turned my head, pretending to still be asleep and squinted through my eyelashes. There was a small, skin headed guy sat, hunched over on the next bed. I couldn't quite see what he was doing as he had his back to me. As I slowly peered round I was horrified. He only had one arm, which wasn't in itself so bad but he had a strap around what was left of it, causing the end to go red and was injecting into the stump! He didn't see me looking so I turned back round. I may be down on my luck but I'm not putting up with that s**t.

I waited there frozen to the spot for what seemed ages then eventually the guy left the room. I went downstairs and complained to staff.

"I am not going to sleep in a room with a scumbag like that! He could come back at night completely off his head and stab me with his dirty needle or anything." I shouted at them. Staff told me to calm down and they would look into it and try and get me moved as soon as possible.

"Fine", I said, unhappy about the prospect of spending the night with a one armed bandit. I hadn't washed for days and was in dire need of a shower. I even had to ask the staff for a towel as I had no stuff with me at all. I did have a suitcase but it was in a locker at the security desk of

'News International'. This was the office building for The Sun and The News of the World newspapers. I would get into the papers soon enough but for now, it was just my bag.

3

Pepto Bismol

Six months earlier, my older brother Jason, who is now a DJ and goes by the name of JFK, had received a phone call from a friend asking if he knew anyone who would be a compere at a lap dancing night in the Meridian Bar, Leicester. Well, my brother immediately thought of me and told his mate that I would do it.

When he told me I thought, yeah, no problem. I had no idea what to do but knew that, once again, I could wing it. When the night came, I went to the venue to meet the girls.

There were three from Newcastle and a couple from London. They all looked pretty much the same, blonde hair, extra white teeth and orange skin like the girls (and some guys) that you see in Boots when you walk past the make-up counter.

I got on quite well with them though and soon we were all snorting coke in the dressing room. We were on such a high, they seemed to love it and after watching them get ready for the show I found myself chatting with two girls in particular. One was Tricky Dee, the main attraction of the night. She was a typical, bleached hair, big boobs, glamour model and had been in a Prodigy video, done a Guinness advert and was regularly in the News of the World exposing her wares. The other girl, Shaz, was the owner of a lap-dancing agency called 'The Rhythmic Angels' in Newcastle. I was trying to get in with all the girls, hoping I could secure another gig. At the end of the evening I had done pretty well and the conversation went onto where they would be performing next and the fact that they didn't have a compere for there either.

Tricky was such a spoilt brat that she demanded I be the compere at the next gig or she wasn't going to do it. I didn't put up a fight. Watching naked girls dancing around and getting paid for it… Well what hot blooded male would say no? Shaz agreed and offered to pay for my flight as their next gig was in Ibiza in two weeks time. I was really excited and didn't want to go home but after a few more beers the night ended and I went back to the pub where I was staying temporarily. The pub was near the centre of Leicester, bang opposite Welford Road Prison and was known for its sporting connections with Leicester Tigers and often some of the rugby team would drink there. It had a small beer garden, a pool room and a couple of lounges. Upstairs were four bedrooms, a lounge and kitchen with a back room that they used for parties.

It was the day before I had to go to Newcastle airport where I was meeting some of the girls for the flight to Ibiza. I'd been on the fruit machine in the pub as usual that day and for some reason had fallen out with Mark, the landlord, over something really petty. It had been blown out of all proportion and the atmosphere had become nasty.

Mark was a big bloke, thick set and very strong with dark short hair and tattoos. He'd confronted me in the pool room and as he had been cooking in the kitchen, still had a knife in his hand. He didn't intend to use it but it still intimidated me. He started shouting at me and I shouted back. He told me to pack my stuff and get out, saying I was a sponger and never would amount to anything. I stormed off to my room on the top floor. He followed me to the floor below and went into the front room. I started to put my stuff in a bag, all the while we were shouting at the tops of our voices calling each other horrible names. I was so angry I couldn't contain it anymore and snapped! I ran downstairs to the front room, smacking him round the face and knocking him to the ground. I pinned him to the floor then, as I stared into his eyes my senses came flooding back. What the hell was I doing? This could get ugly. I looked at the front room door and remembered that the handle had broken off some time before and if you closed it, there was no way in or out without using a screwdriver or knife for a handle. I jumped up, grabbed my bag and ran out slamming the door behind me. I knew I had to get away as quickly as I could. I was afraid of what he might do to me if he didn't have to waste time with the handle but I was more afraid of what I might do to him!

I ran along the corridor letting out a kind of nervous laughter and went downstairs through the pool room into the main bar area of the pub.

You could tell by the punters' faces that they had heard everything that had gone on up there. I made my way to the door thinking I had made good my escape when in walked two police officers. Somebody must have called them. They stopped me in my tracks.

"What's going on here?" one of the officers asked. He was only about five ten in height but was built like a brick s**thouse which made me think twice about barging past him. Immediately I went into victim mode.

"Please help me, this bloke's trying to kill me, he's gone nuts." That second, Mark came bounding into the room and I thought it was going to kick off big time.

"No, no! He's the one causing trouble, I want him out!" he demanded.

There was a brief pause as the two coppers looked at each other then all hell broke loose as we started screaming at each other again. The coppers decided it was best to remove me from the premises and grabbed my arms, frog marching me out the door.

They took me to their car and told me to calm down or I would be arrested then asked me the usual questions, date of birth etc. and if I had somewhere they could drop me as they were not going to leave me there.

I told them that I was now technically homeless.

"All I've got is in this f***ing bag," I yelled and explained that I needed to get to Newcastle, if anywhere, as I had a job to go to. When I told them what it was and what I was going to be doing they looked at each other and said

"Yeah right!"

I asked them to take me to the police station to let me make a call to see if I could resolve the problem and to my surprise they did.

I got there and called Shaz and immediately explained what had happened. I managed to talk her into paying for a taxi from Leicester to Newcastle saying she could take it out of my first wages. I said my farewells to the old bill and left town for what I thought would be bigger and better things.

When I arrived in Ibiza I was met by about twenty girls from different lap-dancing clubs around the UK. Blondes, brunettes, red heads you name it, they were there. I thought it was going to be the best job I had ever had. I introduced myself and we made our way to the apartments together. I had only been there for what seemed like five minutes when the bubble burst. They started bitching at each other, vying for attention and I very quickly realised that working with twenty, self centred, prima donnas, all as f***ed up as I was, was not going to be easy. I soon got into the swing of things though, even with absolutely no money. I started checking out who was who in the bars and clubs and it didn't take long before I noticed that I could get myself a lot of perks because of the attention the girls got when we went out on the town.

I had no problem getting into the V.I.P. areas and many very rich men would ply me with vodka and the white stuff (devils dandruff, coke) just as long as I would get the girls to hang on their every word and make them look good. These guys had serious money, of course, they didn't carry any cash around with them as everything was on account, but you could tell they were loaded by the bling they were wearing and the huge seven foot body guards that watched their every move.

Things seemed ok for a couple of weeks and then my health started to nose dive. My nose was diving into ridiculous amounts of cocaine; I was drinking way too much booze and, as a result, had very little sleep. Then to top it all off, I got 'deli belly' from drinking tap water! I was struggling just to get up every day and when Shaz told me that it was time to go back to England I was ready for it. I felt so rough.

I asked her for my wages but she just laughed. "What wages?" she said. "Who do you think has paid for all your meals and stuff?" I was completely gutted. "F***ing bitch!" I thought, but was too weak to argue with her. She gave me enough for the flight home and then left. I packed my bags and managed to drag my sorry ass to the airport to get the flight. After paying for my ticket home I was completely skint yet again and desperately needed some cash or I would be stuck at the other end with, not only no money but with nowhere to go again. So, as always, I looked for opportunities to keep my head above water, and whilst on the flight, chatted up a Welsh girl called Drew. I tried to persuade her to lend me twenty five quid, vowing I would send it on to her and pay her a visit if she gave me her address. She was a lovely lass with dark brown hair and a broad Welsh accent and after about an hour of relentless charm she gave into me and gave me the money.

I spent the rest of the flight and subsequent train journey to Leicester plying myself with drinks to numb the pain, thanks to Drew. (I never did pay her that visit or send the money to her. Sorry Drew - wherever you are?)

On arrival back home I could only think of one place to go and headed off to one of my old neighbour's flats.

Her name was Judy. She was about fifty years old, small but thickset and was a writer. I had been evicted from the flat next door to her some time earlier for running up bills and not paying the rent. When she opened the door she took one look at me with a fag in her mouth and said,

"You'd better come in." She put me up on her bed settee and nursed me for three days feeding me copious amounts of Pepto Bismol to sort my guts out. It felt like the bottom had fallen out of my world, quite literally! Her flat was small but had everything a single woman of fifty might need. The walls were hidden by shelf after shelf of books and even though it wasn't to my taste she seemed happy there. When my insides started to feel normal again I began thinking of my future. I had no idea what I was going to do or where I would stay long term. Then, one afternoon I got a call from Tricki Dee. She was back in London and had this idea of becoming an actress (fat chance I thought) and, as I had gone to RADA, she asked if I would teach her. I explained my homeless situation to her and she said that I could go and stay with her in her apartment in Chelsea. Bingo!

The ticket inspector was about two carriages away; I sat there nervously racking my brain for a plausible story, I had no ticket and no money. I had jumped the train to London many times before. Sometimes the tickets were never checked and on the odd occasion I got caught. I'd use all sorts of excuses from being mugged to going to see a sick relative in an emergency. Sometimes I even told the truth and depending on the type of person who was working that day I would get various results.

People started getting their tickets ready and I had to make a decision fast. The inspector was a miserable looking git and he wasn't smiling at any of the passengers as he checked their tickets. I didn't fancy taking him on and made a quick dash for the toilet. I'd hidden in the toilet before and got caught but this time I had a new trick up my sleeve.

I went into the loo and stood behind the door with my hand on the handle holding it open so that it gently rocked to and fro with the rhythm of the train. I had noticed before on previous trips that the inspector only knocked on closed toilet doors and hoped that when he saw the door open he would pass by thinking that no one was in there. It was a long shot but I had no other option. "Tickets please" I heard him say. He was really close now and I was s**ting myself (I suppose I was in the right place!). I heard him knock on the toilet door opposite. There was no answer so he opened it. No one was inside. I swallowed hard, expecting the worst.

"Have you got a ticket sir?" I heard him say, half expecting him to come through the door, but he didn't, he was asking someone else. He kept on walking and entered the next carriage continuing his round! I let out a huge sigh. It had worked. I couldn't relax yet though or stay in there for that matter. I peered round the door to see if all was clear and left the loo looking for a recently vacated seat with a table. Luckily I found one with a discarded ticket on top so I picked it up and held it face down with enough of the ticket showing to give the impression I had a valid one, then pretended to be asleep. My heart was still beating like a drum and my body was pumping adrenaline but after a couple of minutes my breathing calmed down and a smug grin spread across my face. "I don't know how you do it Johnny Kinch". I thought. I'd done it again!

4

Getting cold

Friday night, and by the time I got to Tricki's I needed a drink. I rang the doorbell and she welcomed me with her fake smile and her even more fake boobs. She was always scantily clad; trying to show off her assets and today was no exception. She showed me to my room and I unpacked my suitcase then took a shower. She'd planned for us to go to 'Stringfellows' that night and to the 'K bar' in Chelsea the following evening. So after a few shots of vodka we made our way to 'Stringfellows' in the West End.

I had been there many years before with a mate called Jonnie Cave but this time round I was treated well and had plenty of free booze as I knew most of the girls from my stint in Ibiza. Good job too, as I would have needed to take out a mortgage to cover the cost of the over priced drinks. The music was banging and the club was full of wanabes. The birds were practically naked and all over the blokes like cheap suits. The guys couldn't get enough of it and were stuffing twenty-pound notes into their G-strings to show their appreciation. Every single person in there only wanted to know you if you had money and guess what? I was skint! I kind of felt out of place because of that and after a couple of hours wanted to get out of there but my problem was Tricki was the only one with money so I was completely reliant on her. I hated the fact I could never make my own decisions because I was living out of someone else's pocket. One day things would go my way and I would call the shots.

That night was a late one and when we got back I lay there wide awake, buzzing from the coke and with a million and one thoughts going round my head. I must have dropped off at some point and after lounging around all the next day, recovering, we got ready and headed off to the 'K bar'. We pulled up outside in a taxi. I was wearing all black and looked pretty cool and Tricki had on the usual attire, which was basically anything that would draw people's attention away from her tiny empty brain and down to her enormous breasts.

The paparazzi were outside the club, trying to get shots of celebrities and two huge doormen were protecting a camp looking guy with a clipboard who was checking if people were on the guest list. Tricki preened herself and we got out of the cab and walked over to the main door. Thankfully we were on the list and in we went, no problems. It was really dark inside and was nothing special. I was quite disappointed after Tricki had been going on all day about how exclusive it was. After a couple of drinks, the coke and conversation started flowing freely (In that order). People were dancing and we were all having a great time.

I got chatting to loads of people because of the coke. You see, when I was out of it I could talk for England, my mates even called me Mike Tyson as I'd chew everyone's ears off when I got going. I was stood at the bar with my mouth going ten to the dozen and could tell the person I was talking to thought I was nuts so I decided to have a look around the place. There were little recesses in the walls which led to small candle lit rooms where people could talk more intimately. I was about to go in one when I noticed a familiar face in the corner of the room. Full of confidence from the coke, I went over to talk to him. It was Mark Owen from 'Take That'. He looked kind of sad, although, I dread to think what I looked like. I sat down at his table and introduced myself and we got talking.

It turned out he was down in London to see his record company. He had been staying in the Lake District in a house near his granny where he was trying to write an album to make a comeback. He said the record company wouldn't agree to any of his songs, they were too dark. I was quite surprised as to how normal he was. He seemed a really nice guy. I didn't want to over stay my welcome (probably for the first time in my life) and after about ten minutes I left him alone. He eventually did make a comeback but I'm sure it wasn't the way he expected. I'm really happy for him now that he's doing so well with the renewed success of 'Take That'. There's a lesson to be learnt there. Even when we think things are totally finished, if we just hang on in there long enough, we just might get a second bite of the cherry. Well done Mark!

Anyway, after a while I went outside to cool down. It was a lovely night and I was just about to light a cigarette when a guy came over to me and asked if I had come there with Tricki Dee. I looked at him inquisitively and he reached into his pocket.

"Here, take my card, I'm a freelance reporter." he said. "If you have any gossip you can get cash for confessions. If you ever get any dirt on her, give me a call and we can talk." Now, if I'd have actually liked her I would have told him where to get off but never one to miss an opportunity I discreetly took his card and went back inside to drink the night away.

The next day it all went pear shaped. I felt like s**t from all the poison running round in my body and to add insult to injury, Tricky came in all guns blazing.

"How could you tell my boyfriend that I had been playing around in Ibiza?" she screamed at me. She had obviously spoken to him that morning and he must have let slip what I had told him in confidence. "What the f**k are you talking about you spoilt t**t?" I yelled back in denial. I was still full of coke and drink so just let rip at her, but then I was never one to hold my tongue anyway. Just who the hell was she to talk to me like I was a piece of s**t. I wasn't going to stand for it. I didn't care who she thought she was but yet again I wasn't in a position to call the shots; if she kicked me out I was stuffed.

"How dare you talk to me like that. You're a nobody! I want you out now!" she screamed at me, then turned to her fella; "I want him out now!" He was quite a big lad with dark hair, good looks and a strong South African accent. He was trying to calm her down whilst telling me to go. I just ignored them both and sat down which made things worse and she stormed off out of the room and called the police. I was determined that I wasn't going anywhere; after all I had been given a key and wrongly thought that gave me some sort of rights.

The police arrived within minutes and two male coppers got out their car and came to the front door. I may have stood a chance if one of them had been a woman but with two blokes and the way Tricky looked I was f***ed. She went straight into her hurt dumb blonde routine and wrapped them round her little finger; I didn't stand a chance,

"Ok Miss, leave it to us" one of the pigs said, ordering me to leave the premises.

"I've got nowhere to go and no money" I snapped at them. "Leave or be arrested" they said in unison. "Leave it Johnny" I thought, trying to stop myself smacking one of them in the gob. They were just a couple of pigs, wet behind the ears and straight out of police academy.

"Right f**k this" I said grabbing my suitcase, "I hope you die you sad cow" I bellowed out as I dragged my case down the hallway. What the hell was I going to do now? However, it was only seconds before my mind was sifting through ideas and then I remembered the card I had been given by the reporter at the 'K bar'. My mind was like that, it seemed to work best when I was under pressure and no matter what s**t I got myself into I was confident that I would come out on top. I had a couple of quid to make a few calls and while I was leaving I was already putting together a story that I hoped I could sell to the papers.

The coppers followed me in their car to the end of the street. I stopped every now and then when I was too tired to carry on and turned round to look at them. They just sat and stared back, so I flicked the V's and shouted "B*****ks to you lot, I'm out of here!"

I walked into a pub under a bridge and looked around. My suitcase must have been a give-away to the reporter I'd arranged to meet.

"Johnny?" he said signalling me with his eyebrows and holding out a business card.

"Are you the guy from the papers?" I asked.

"Yeah, my name's Tom" he replied. He was dressed in a tired looking suit with a scrunched up tie and a shirt that wouldn't pass the Daz test. He wasn't much older than I was and when we'd sat down he looked at me through a pair of large metal rimmed glasses and said,

"So what do you know?" Still full of anger and betrayal I went into a tirade of accusations slagging off Tricki Dee, trying to get the reporter interested in what I had to say. At least I might get a couple of pints out of him and a few quid.

I told him about the flowing cocaine, the parties and a whole load of other stuff and he seemed very interested. We ended up having four or five pints during which, he called his boss who told him to bring me down to their office at 'News International' in White City.

We took a cab there and walked into the main reception where he told me to wait while he went to speak to his boss.

There were a couple of security guards on duty and when Tom the reporter had gone, I showed them his business card and asked if there was anywhere I could store my case and use the toilet. They said it was no problem and that they could put my case in a locker and I could fetch it when I wanted. Before I stashed it I went into the toilets and thought I'd better put on something warm and comfortable, it was November and getting colder. I had moved so many times in my life and most of them at a moments notice. What with my drink, drugs and gambling problems, it was always going to be just a matter of time before I found myself in this situation again.

The reception area was quite small with a couple of sofas, a fish tank and a TV in the corner that constantly showed the news. I sat there, waiting, watching the fish go round. As the time went by I became less and less optimistic about the possibility of getting some cash for my story. Then the reporter came back! I got a little rush of butterflies as he took me into a side room. He explained that they were interested but only if I was prepared to go back and capture any untoward behaviour on a hidden camera. I thought about it and knowing that Tricki knew some pretty nasty people I said no.

"No problem mate ... Listen, good luck and take care of yourself, I hope this helps" he said standing up and holding out twenty quid. I thanked him and took the money, shaking his hand.

"Well that was quick" I said and walked out the door. So now I'd got twenty quid, no baggage to weigh me down and that was the end of that. I guess I'll have to find another way to make it!

It was a beautiful night. The air was crisp and I could see the lights of London glimmering on the Thames as I made my way down the embankment. I didn't know where I was going or what was going to happen that night but one thing was for sure, I was convinced that there was more for me in life than this and I was determined to find out what it was.

5

Scooby doo

I took my towel and went to the showers. I love having a shower, the more powerful the better. I like it when it feels like someone is chucking a bucket of nails on your back, which's when I know it's strong enough. I stayed in there for ages trying to wash away my recent problems. "Ah… bliss," I said as the water massaged my back. Just a s**t, shower and shave and I was ready to go.

After a few days of running around letting the different agencies know that my address was now the hostel and after successfully applying for a crisis loan, I started settling in. I was moved to the eighth floor and put in a room with a guy nick-named 'Tommy' because of the fake 'Tommy Hilfiger' cap he always wore.

He was in his late twenties with short brown hair and a pale complexion and thought he was a right wide boy, a proper cockney. Like me he had a few issues and his main drug of choice was 'Blues' (Diazepam) or 'Scooby doo's', as they were known. They were fairly easy to get hold of and were split into three groups, white 2mg, yellow 5mg and blue 10mg. They'd really chill you out when you were clucking, (term used for heroin addicts as the drugs wore off), but not just for that, they had helped me out big time on many occasions when I was feeling strung out. One time I remember feeling so desperate I was convinced that there was no way out other than taking my own life. This thought just wouldn't go away. It was like an ache in my mind. Every few minutes it would pop in my head and it felt like something or someone was trying to take me out. I just wanted the pain and loneliness to stop. I was afraid that my mental health was going downhill so fast that it wasn't a case of if but more like *when* I would do it. I had been binge drinking, coming down from the coke and my head was buzzing with a million and one thoughts telling me that I'd never amount to anything, that I was doomed to a lifetime of bad luck and that this was my lot in life. I was full of negativity and no matter how hard I tried to push the thoughts away they were too strong and just kept coming back again. I was helpless to do anything about it. I had no power over them and they controlled my mind.

I didn't know what to do and needed to talk to someone, anyone, then I thought of my dad.

I sluggishly went down stairs to the phone booth outside the hostel and called him. I didn't know who else to turn to and like a child away from home I wanted reassurance from my father. The phone booth was right next to the road, one of those small shoulder height ones that didn't have any privacy. I huddled up inside, trying to get as close to the sound-absorbing panel as possible, so no-one could hear how weak I was feeling. It probably seems weird but it was a small part of the whole survival thing. If anyone found any weakness they could assume I was a push over and start giving me grief and that's the last thing I needed right now. My Dad answered and I blurted some stuff out to him about killing myself and he tried to give me words of encouragement but nothing could penetrate the wave of negativity swamping my mind. I'm sure he felt as helpless as I did. When I put the phone down, tears streamed down my face and I felt totally lost. Then suddenly, I remembered I'd got two yellows (5mg Diazepam) in my room. They were my only hope of some sort of peace that night, so I ran up stairs burst through the door searching frantically for them but it was no good I couldn't find them anywhere. I sat on the bed exhausted "Where the f**k are they then" I said in defeat. Then out the corner of my eye I saw them on top of the wardrobe, I jumped up and grabbed them "Thank God for that" I said opening the bottle and throwing them down my neck.

I'd had enough that day and collapsed on the bed hoping that I would make it through the night without dying. Oh, how I dreamed of waking up without depression and with a clear mind. But that seemed like a distant unreachable dream and right now I had to take it moment by moment. Ten minutes later my breathing slowed down and my thoughts, as chaotic as they were, started to dissipate. For now at least I had forgotten about killing myself, in fact I didn't feel much at all. There was now calm where there was once chaos, but as blissful as it was I knew in the back of my mind that it was only temporary, but at that point I didn't care and sank into a deep sleep.

6

Kfs

There were about 70 blokes in the hostel varying in age between 18 and 65 and nearly all had some level of drug or alcohol dependency. If you didn't have an addiction before you went in, you certainly would have by the time you left! There was no one in the hostel as physically as strong as me, the majority of the guys were heroin dependant and most of them 'mainlined' (that's injected to you and me), which made them thinner and weaker. Their bones would become brittle and their immune system would shut down, so normally if any of them got shirty with me they would soon back down when I threatened to smash their heads in. I very quickly realised that I didn't have the added worry of watching my back all the time, which afforded me a certain freedom.

I loved being in the centre of London. I could literally walk out the door and round the corner onto Neal Street and it would feel like I was a million miles away from the doom and gloom of the hostel. There were so many shops, all full of gorgeous clothes and fancy footwear. "If I had the money I would be the best dressed bloke in London" I used to tell myself. London was so fast paced, people were going here and there; everyone was so driven, time was money! I was used to moving around in the hustle and bustle so it strangely seemed like home to me.

One evening when I was feeling restless I went for a walk through Soho. The rain had just stopped and it was quite humid. I approached Soho square and I started to think about the mess I was in. Soho was a weird place, there were so many different types of people there and when I turned the corner I saw a young chap sat on the kerb in the street. He was sat crossed legged and had a lighter in his right hand which was lit and he was holding it under a spoon cooking up what I can only im-agine was heroin. As I stood at a distance and watched him I looked to the opposite side of the road and my eyes fell on a completely different scene. A young couple were sat in a posh candle lit restaurant sipping wine and enjoying a meal together blissfully unaware of what was taking place only feet from where they were sitting. Unbelievable.

Then as I was thinking it dawned on me that I couldn't be placed with either group. I was somewhere in the middle and in reality nearer the bottom than the top. "What a f**king strange world we live in" I thought.

Things just kind of ticked along for the next few weeks, every day seemed like Groundhog Day. I would wake up early morning grab my cup and KFS (knife fork spoon) and make my way down the eight flights of stairs to the basement for breakfast where the kitchen and dining room were.

Breakfast was always minging. The bacon looked like it had been taken from a diseased pig and was always cold. "I wouldn't give this to a dog" I sneered loud enough for the staff to hear, but having no other choice, I'd eat it, then smuggle as much bread out as possible for later consumption and go back to bed until about 10.30 am. Then I'd get up and check the mail list in reception, to see who had been paid a giro that day. This made it easier for me to tap them up for a few quid, so I could have a drink and a couple of bets. If that didn't work I would go rob something from a shop and sell it in the bookies. Best sellers were razors (Gillette mach 3) which used to be easy to get from high street stores or mobile phones, which were even easier to pick up in bars if you had the balls to do it.

By the time for the evening meal at about 5.30 pm I had probably made 50-60 quid but lost the lot in the bookies. Horses, dogs, it didn't really matter I'd bet on whatever I could.

After tea I'd play pool for cigarettes then maybe go on the scrounge trying to get enough together for a couple of cans of strong lager. I would sit with all the other alcoholics and consume the cans until the flow stopped or I was too tired to stay awake whichever one came first. This would go on and on for weeks. One day I was chatting with Blackie, one of the long-term residents. He was about five foot ten with curly dark hair and limped around on crutches due to some problems with his legs. He was an alcoholic in the full sense of the word and also HIV positive. To stop other drunks catching AIDS from him he would cover his bottle of cider with black gaffer tape then write the letters HIV on the side in tippex. It wasn't that he was socially responsible but it ensured that no one would nick his drink when he'd passed out in the street. Normally you couldn't catch it by drinking from the same bottle but his gums were like an open wound and when talking to him you would regularly see the gaps where his teeth used to be weeping with blood and pus. It wasn't a pretty sight but we all had our problems and although on the outside I looked fine, on the inside I was as bad if not worse than he was. He told me that I could sign on and sell the Big Issue, which if done well, could apparently be quite lucrative. "Why hadn't anyone told me that before?" I said to him.

I knew that the people I had seen out on the street selling it looked like s**t and never really made an effort to actually connect with any passers by. They just played on the fact that some people have a conscience and only got sales from those that pitied them. I was different though; I'd got charm and talent and knew with a bit of luck I could make a killing at this. "Maybe, just maybe, if I could earn enough to place a huge bet and win big, this could be my way out," I thought like all gamblers do. I was always looking for the next free ride. I had hardly ever done any real work in my life and thought I would probably stay on the dole until one day, from nowhere, my luck would change and I would make it big time or I would drop dead.

I wanted fame and fortune so much and, although selling the Big Issue was hardly fame and fortune it would hopefully put some cash in my pocket and afford me the luxuries I thought I deserved. I went to the main Big Issue office in Kings Cross and signed up.

It was full of people doing exactly the same thing and I had to wait in a great big bloody queue. Once the queue had gone down and I had got my official i.d. card from them, I was given 10 free copies to start me off then assigned a pitch from which to sell.

My pitch was outside a Prêt a Manger near Holborn tube station. It was perfect, really busy through out the morning and when lunchtime arrived someone would come out of the sandwich shop and give me dinner.

I couldn't bring myself to just stand there though looking sad like the rest of them so I had to come up with something different.

First thing when I got there I thumbed through the mag looking for inspiration and to be honest it didn't look much good, the only saving grace was that it was a special anniversary edition celebrating their 7th year of publication and you got a free CD.

"Big Issue! Big Issue! Get this week's special edition with a naked poster of Kylie! Big tissue, big tissue!" I shouted out tongue in cheek. I got the odd laugh from passers by and a few bought one. "This is easy," I thought and before long I sold all ten at a pound each and rushed back to buy some more.

They cost me 40 pence a pop and as the day went on I made about 70 quid. I couldn't believe it. This was too easy. When I thought I had earnt enough for the day I headed straight for the bookies. Seven hours it took me to make it and 20 minutes to lose it.

I couldn't believe it "what a t**t," I said to myself. I didn't even have enough left for a couple of cheap beers and so the cycle of earn, lose, scrounge would continue over and over again. On some days I would stand on top of a post box and recite Shakespeare's sonnets, offering a personal one to one recital in return for a sale.

People loved to see someone selling the Big Issue with a smile on their face and would often stop and pay me double the price to hear a sonnet even though they didn't want a magazine. It was a win-win situation for me, but of course, at the end of every day I had nothing to show for my efforts and slowly but surely my endless struggle brought on depression making my moods become increasingly erratic.

I didn't hang around with anyone in particular at the hostel, as I didn't feel we were on the same level. Of course we all had similar needs and problems, but I felt that I was going to get out of all this s**t and rise above it one day. "They" seemed to be content with merely existing. I wanted to live and live to the max. I guess it was a bit like the TV sitcom 'Only Fools and Horses', always chasing the dream but never fully realising it. "This time next year we'll be millionaires" as Del boy used to say, but they never quite made it and when they did they lost it all. What made it worse for me was the fact that this wasn't a sitcom and no happy ending was scripted. This was for real but I was determined not to give up just yet. I would write my own ending!

Gambling was now a huge problem for me; it started off small by putting just a few quid in the bandits on a Friday and Saturday night down the pub, losing that then sticking all my wages in to try and claw it back. Another time a mate of mine Paul Sharp took me to a bookie and I put £5 on a horse at 7/2 and it won. I got £22.50 back. I couldn't believe it. I was instantly hooked.

I started betting bigger and bigger amounts not really noticing that it had become a habit and was snowballing out of control. I'd always run out of money and end up borrowing off people to fuel my growing addiction by making up incredibly elaborate stories to convince them to part with their cash and 99% of the time, it worked. I thought I was invincible and even though at the time I genuinely believed I'd pay them back as promised I hardly ever did. People had sussed me out as I was letting them down more and more regularly, so much so that I had to move as a result of the threats I was getting. I couldn't go anywhere without someone hassling me for the money I owed them. It was a nightmare and I knew it was gonna get me into trouble but I just couldn't stop myself.

7

Much ado about nothing

"What on earth are you doing selling the Big Issue, you should be on the stage," said a regular customer passing by on his lunch break. "Tell me about it," I shouted back. I stopped and thought for a moment. It was ironic, I'd been on the stage many times before and hoped and dreamed of being there again one day. It was strange him saying that today of all days. It was the 12th September 1998, and two years ago to the day I was getting ready to move to London to hit the big time. I'd been accepted as a student at The Royal Academy of Dramatic Art (RADA) and was convinced that after my bad luck this was my ticket to stardom.

I'd auditioned all that year, at places like the Bristol Old Vic Theatre school, Central School of Speech and Drama and, of course, RADA in London. I'd been turned down by two of the schools but knew from the start that RADA was the place for me. I sent off my application form and audition fee of £25 and waited impatiently for a confirmation letter or an invitation to audition. When it finally came I was over the moon and began learning my chosen pieces in earnest. At my first audition I had to perform a piece from a Shakespeare play and then sing unac-companied in front of a panel of West End Judges who were made up of a Director, a playwright and a member of the board at RADA I chose to read Maralus, a character from Shakespeare's Julius Caesar and for my song chose Tom Lehrer's, "Poisoning Pigeons in the Park", which went down a storm. I was as nervous as hell though. I remember feeling so anxious whilst waiting for my turn that I started hyperventilating and must have gone to the loo about twenty times to empty my bowels. After all that waiting and nervousness the audition flew by and I really enjoyed myself in there. I couldn't believe how well it went and left the building. I felt on top of the world. I was so focused I didn't even notice it was raining outside. As I strode off down the road I heard someone shouting "Jonathan Jonathan!" I turned round to see one of the female judges from the audition panel beckoning me back to the building.

"Hi," I shouted, making my way back. I thought maybe I had left something in the room but to my surprise she told me they were so impressed with my audition they wanted to offer me a call back there and then and put me out of my misery instead of having to wait for four weeks to hear from them. You should have seen the grin on my face I was over the moon and was now convinced that I was in, even though I still had a further two auditions to get through before I could be sure. Me being me and wanting this so badly I told everyone that I'd already been accepted and had been given a place.

I practiced really hard during the few months before my next audition, going over and over the scripts until I could say them in my sleep. Then when the time came I stepped up to the mark and somehow sailed through with flying colours. I was on a roll and all I needed to do now was get through the final one and as far as I was concerned my future was in the bag.

The last audition came and went. It was very much like the others and went well but this time I didn't hear anything for ages and started to get a bit down, so I thought I'd give them a call to see if there was any news. "Royal Academy of Dramatic Art" said a lady with a cockney accent.

"Hi my name is Johnny Kinch, I'm just calling to find out if I got through my last audition. It was for a place on the three year acting course."

"Hold please," she said. I waited a couple of seconds then a man's voice came on the line "Hello Jonathan, Nicholas Barter here, Principal. Where on earth have you been? We have been trying to get hold of you; did you receive the letter we sent you?"

"No." I said.

"Well its good news we would like to offer you a place on this year's course." I went silent for a couple of seconds "No way!" I screamed down the phone "That's fantastic!" I had done it. Somehow I had beaten off thousands of other applicants from around the world and I, Johnny Kinch had won one of fifteen male places at RADA.

"No more slumming it for me," I thought. "Surely my time had come." Finally someone had recognised the raw talent I had and now I was going to be polished into the finished article.

"Your not quite there yet though," said the principal reining my excitement in. "There's still the little matter of raising your fees. Have you got any funding yet?"

"No." I said.

"Don't worry," he said, "We have arranged for you to go on BBC Radio Leicester and they're going to interview you about how you got in and then discuss with you the lack of funding for the arts, so just be yourself and you might get some sponsors from it ok?"

"Ok no probs," I said.

Things went pretty quickly from that point on, I was so excited and wrote loads of letters to various companies asking for sponsorship but all I got was a big fat no! Then one day I received a letter from 'Laura Ashley' the retail outlet.

They wrote *"Thank you for your recent letter for sponsorship, we have never sponsored the Arts before and would like to invite you to London for an interview and audition. We were very impressed with your letter and were moved by the fact that the whole letter was written in capitals except for when you used the letter "i" referring to yourself. By doing this we could see that you clearly felt for many years you were of less worth than your peers."*

I'd completely forgotten about that letter as it was so bad and thanked my lucky stars that they had got it so wrong. You see I had never typed a thing in my life before that and when I wrote the letter I had used an old word processor. The only problem was, that all the letters were stuck in capitals except the letter 'i' which was stuck in lower case. But hey, what did I care? I'd had my first positive response and immediately got to work on my audition piece; I needed to raise about forty grand so it was essential to seize every opportunity.

I arrived in London and made my way to the address given on the letter. "Right this is it," I said as I climbed the stairs heading for reception. "Hi, my name's Johnny, I'm here for an interview." I said looking the receptionist in the eyes and smiling.

"Hi," she replied, "have a seat over there and they'll call you when they are ready."

It was a beautiful day and the sun was shining in through the windows throwing shafts of light across the room. I sat down feeling that things were finally going my way.

"You can go in now," said the receptionist pointing to the door opposite. I had a newly found confidence thanks to my previous auditions and an air of invincibility about me. I got up and breezed in the room like

I owned the place. "Hi I'm Johnny," I said going straight over to shake everyone's hand. There were four people on the interviewing panel two men and two women. The blokes had grey hair and one was wearing a cravat and the two ladies were impeccably dressed like they'd just walked off a 1940's film set. They were all quite old and one of the ladies looked suspiciously like the silhouette of the lady on the front of all the Laura Ashley shops. I'm still convinced it was her.

"So far so good," I thought. They were all still smiling and seemed to enjoy my cocky diamond geezer type of approach to the whole situation. I sat down and they asked a series of questions, which thankfully I had the right answers to. It was going so well I even cracked a few jokes and before I knew it, it was time to perform my audition pieces.

Without any hesitation I walked to the middle of the room and got on with it. You should have seen their faces, they loved it!

This time I was acting the part of Benedict from Shakespeare's 'Much Ado About Nothing' and I sang a song called 'Buddy can you spare a dime.' Little did I know just how poignant that title would become later. I had got those two pieces down to a T and when I finished they gave out a fitting round of applause, which was great as normally at auditions no matter how good you were all you got were staring eyes and the odd wry smile. I was then asked to leave the room while they chatted so I went back to reception where I was given a hot drink and a biscuit. I sat for a while sipping my tea and going over it again in my mind just to see if I could remember any signs of disapproval on their faces. Then after about ten minutes the receptionist said "They've finished deliberating and are ready for you now, if you'd like to go back in?" "Ok, thanks," I answered. "Your not as cocky now," I thought to myself as I sat down in front of them. "Firstly, well done," the lady who looked like Laura Ashley said in an extremely well spoken but gentle voice. "We know it can't be easy doing what you've just done in front of total strangers." There was a long pause as we all smiled at each other. "So how do you think it went?" she asked. "Good. It went well and er I hope you all er enjoyed it?" I stuttered.

"Yes we did," she replied. "In fact we enjoyed it immensely and were really impressed with your Benedict, which happens to be one of my favourite Shakespearean characters and without further ado," she said letting out a little giggle, "We are going to award you with fifteen thousand pounds! What do you think about that?" Trying not to leap out of my chair and ten feet in the air I simply said with jaw dropping "You're joking."

"No we are not joking," came the reply "and if this works out with you, we are going to do this for others too," she said.

Well I didn't care about the others but I wasn't going to tell them that. "That's fantastic," I exclaimed as she handed me a 'Coutts and Co' cheque for my first instalment of 5K. They had already done all the checking up they needed with RADA to verify I actually had a place on the acting course and everything had checked out, so they had no problem giving me the cheque there and then, and besides I wasn't going to go and blow it... was I?

I left there in shock and amazement no one had ever believed in me that much. I started thinking about what I was going to do with the cheque. I didn't have a bank account at the time so I couldn't put it in a bank to clear just yet, besides I had a million and one other things to do.

There was the radio interview and I had an audition/interview with Leicester Arts Council as they awarded a one off grant each year to the best applicant. I had all these things to think about on my journey home but right now I didn't care all I could think about was stardom.

I was really busy over the next few weeks and things went really well with the radio program. Amazingly, after hearing my plea for sponsors, Sue Townsend (Author of Adrian Mole) called the station and pledged five thousand pounds towards my cause!

It was incredible. But not only that, some weeks later after auditioning for Leicester Arts Council I received another letter awarding me eighteen thousand pounds for fees etc. I had beaten all the applicants there as well. I couldn't believe my luck and as every day went by confidence in my own abilities grew and grew. I was now totally convinced that it was only a matter of time before my name would be in lights!

8

Let's have it

I moved down to London with my Mum and Aunt's words ringing in my ears, "Don't cock this one up like you have everything else." I begrudged those words yet there was truth in them. I think that's why they hurt so much; I knew that I had cocked so many things up in the past that there was always the potential of me doing it again. Was I so predictable?

A mate of mine took me to London in his car. We jammed it so full of stuff we could hardly see out the windows and after a few hours driving we were unpacking my gear into the halls of residence.

I was one of the first students to live in halls (Bonham-Carter house), an old student nurses' residence next door to the RADA building on Gower St in the West End.

It was a great big building with hundreds of rooms and loads of communal kitchens that each landing would share. My room was small and had a tiny sink, a single bed and a built in wardrobe. It looked out onto Mallet Street where there was a theatre called the Vanborough, also owned by RADA. When we'd finished unpacking I waved my mate off and went to have a look around in the main RADA building.

There was a woman on reception who I'd met before whilst auditioning, she asked how I was doing and we got chatting for a couple of minutes. Her name was Val; she had mousy coloured hair and wore glasses. She was a real cockney lass but was very welcoming; made you feel like you'd known her for ages. After chatting for a couple of minutes the principal came out of his office opposite and walked over to us. "Hi Jonathan you're early", he said, "how was your journey?"

"Good thanks" I replied.

"Well I'm glad you're here," he said. "I've got someone I'd like you to meet." At that moment a rather small chap with grey receding hair and glasses came out of the same office "Jonathan, this is Lord Atten-borough" said the principal. I knew who he was I had been watching him in Jurassic Park only a couple of days earlier. I went bright red and didn't know what to say.

"Hello Jonathan and where are you from," asked Lord Attenbor-ough,

"Err, I'm from Leicester," I replied.

"Up the Tigers!" he said back with excitement in his voice referring to the Rugby team "And welcome to RADA," he said "let me show you around," and whisked me off on a personal tour of the building.

He took me to a book that was framed in a glass case with lots of dates and peoples names in it and pointed out his own. It was a list of some of the first people to go to RADA and he had been there way back in 1942. Then we went upstairs to the canteen and had a cup of tea and a chat. "I don't believe this," I thought, "Only a week ago I was scrounging money to get a bag of chips now I'm having tea with Lord Attenborough!" If this was anything to go by I was going to like London and the fame it could bring!

The next day I went to the Halifax building society and opened an account. I knew it was going to be extremely dangerous for me to have such easy access to all this money and to make matters worse when I put the first cheque in from Laura Ashley I was told that because it was a 'Coutts and Co' cheque I could draw on it straight away. You see 'Coutts and Co' were so well regarded it was practically the bank of England.

"How much can I have," I said eagerly

"Up to a thousand pounds," came the answer from the cashier?

"That will do nicely," I replied.

I signed the slip and she counted out the cash, I couldn't believe it I had never seen that kind of money before. I stuffed it in my pocket and left the bank. As I walked out of the door onto Tottenham Court Road I could see a William Hill bookmakers directly across the street and without hesitation thought "Come on let's have it," I was convinced my time had come and with my recent run of luck wrongly thought that if I bet big I could win big and off I went.

The bookies were below ground level cutting out all light so you never knew just how long you'd been in there. Many times I would be in there so long that the staff would change shift. The betting shops had their fair share of low lifes, most of whom didn't have a job. The ones that did would usually lose them along with their families and of course all their money. There are always five or six screens on the wall so you can watch more than one race at a time making sure you will always have some way of losing your money. There were small tables with chairs attached to them where you could sit and write out your betting slips. They would normally be colour coded in each different bookies, like red chairs and tables in Ladbrokes and blue in William Hill. This wasn't the kind of place you would go for a laugh. As I looked around I watched old men pick fag ends up off the floor. I thought "I'm never going to end up like that!"

As soon as I'd checked out the betting and found a horse I wanted to back I started gambling in earnest.

Gambling was like a drug to me; I loved it and yet hated it in the same breath. I'd always bet whatever I'd got and when I had the cash would risk everything leaving myself with nothing and today was no exception. I believed then and still do now that if you're going to do something give 110% or don't bother at all. My first bet was 200 quid on a 6/4 favourite and boy did it get stuffed, it might as well have had three legs. "F**king donkey," I said out loud getting nods of approval from other losing punters. And so on it went, bet after bet and nearly every one went down.

I got the odd winner but only when I was down to my last hundred but even then I'd only win a few quid and never enough to satisfy me or fill the seemingly bottomless void I had inside. I screwed up my last betting slip and threw it in the bin even though the horse was still running.

"Got a spare fag mate," I asked a fellow punter.

"Yeah, here you go," he replied and gave me a light. He looked just as sad as me and when I looked in his eyes they were dark and hollow almost as if he had given up. I took a long deep drag and watched the screen, screwing up my hands and banging on the table. I shouted "Come on you t**t whip him!" My heart was beating so hard it felt like it was gonna jump out my chest at any minute. My horse was about twenty lengths clear coming to the final fence with jockey Adrian Maguire on board, then suddenly everything was silent. "Oh no f**king hell!" I shouted at the top of my voice.

It looked like he didn't even try to jump the fence. He just ploughed through it and collapsed in a heap on the floor. "He never wins for me, p***k!" I yelled. My heart sank and I stood there in disbelief. I had no money left and sat down quietly for a couple of minutes trying to pick myself up, yet again.

Then I remembered I had all that money in the bank. Suddenly my energy came rushing back and I was gone, vaulting the stairs like a young buck, running out of the bookies across the busy street and straight into the bank. Inside there was a massive queue and I was at the back of it, "Come on," I growled "I haven't got all day; some of us have got work to go to." Of course I didn't have but to me what I had to do was more important than work and when something was in the way of one of my habits I could very easily flip and lash out. I'd use any tactic necessary to manipulate others to get my own way.

"Next please," said the cashier after what seemed like an eternity. It was my turn. "Hi, how you doing today?" I said trying to give the impression I was in control of myself. She smiled back at me "What can I do for you sir?" I handed over a withdrawal slip I had filled out whilst waiting, it was for another grand "I'd like to make a withdrawal," I said in a gentle quiet voice.

"Ok sir, just one second," she typed a few details into the computer then said "Oh sorry sir, it's saying that you have withdrawn your maximum for the day."

"I beg your pardon?" I snapped raising my voice. "Are you telling me that I can't withdraw my money out of my account?" emphasising the words my. She looked at me her eyes wide open, surprised that I had suddenly turned on her. "I want to speak to the manager!" I yelled. "I'll be sat over there," pointing to some chairs in the corner and making my way over to them. I'd just sat down when a smart looking chap in a suit with short brown neatly combed hair walked over to me. "Can I help you sir?" he said. "I am the manager."

"Can we talk about this in private?" I asked, "I'm a bit upset."

"Of course," he replied. He took me off into a side room; there were a couple of chairs in there with a monitor and a keyboard. We sat down facing each other over the desk.

"What seems to be the problem?" he asked.

"Well, I made a withdrawal earlier," I said "and that money was supposed to go to pay for my accommodation. I'm new to London you see, I'm a student at RADA and, well I've been and paid that thousand pounds for my accommodation fee and was expecting to receive a couple of hundred pounds from the bursar at college to tide me over so I could get all the essentials I needed to move into halls; microwave, iron, food and all that kind of stuff but they won't let me and now you're telling me

I can't have any money out of my bank account. So as you can see, I'm right in the s**t and I've got no food or anything." I lowered my head and tried to look dejected.

"I'm sorry Mr Kinch but you have reached your daily limit and the cheque hasn't even cleared yet." the manager said, but I wasn't going to give in without a fight. "Come on mate," I begged, "you must have been a student before and know what it's like on the breadline. I've had a really tough time recently and would really appreciate it if you would just help me out this once; I swear I won't ask you again." I could sense that he was breaking and continued trying to wear him down. "I know the computer says that I'm at my limit but as a manager surely you have power over what the computer says. Please, just this once."

I stopped there as I didn't want to over do it. There was a short pause and a sigh from him. "Ok," he said "this once but I'm only giving you three hundred pounds and I shouldn't be doing that, ok?"

"No, that's great!" I replied.

I filled out a new slip and was given the money. "Thanks mate, I appreciate that," I said in triumph and off I went. I got outside onto the busy street and took a deep breath. "You only just got away with that one so don't blow it this time. Right, now let's see if I can win my money back," I said.

As I crossed the street I passed a cash machine that was beeping loudly. I looked over and to my surprise there was fifty pounds sticking out of it. I took a quick look left and right and grabbed it before it was retracted and made my way back down the stairs to the bookies next door. Some unlucky git, probably from the bookies, must have left it whilst in a hurry to get back to the races.

"Wow, fifty quid!" I said to myself, "that is a good sign," and with that started betting almost immediately. Surprisingly, the first few bets won "Yeah, come on that's more like it!" I yelled convinced that finding that money was some sort of omen.

"I didn't think he was going to get there," I said to the cashier as I collected my winnings.

"There you go, two hundred pounds," she said. I took the money and without so much as a thank you, ran over to a table and quickly wrote out a betting slip for the next dog race which was just about to start. That's how it was, I would write out bets without even checking in the papers whether what I was betting on had a chance of winning or not. You see to me deep down inside I thought I was special and believed that one day if I could just hang on in there my ship would come in.

This went on and on for the next few hours, betting on donkeys and losing then finding a rich vein of winning form and everything I touched turned to gold. At one point I'd even won all the money back from earlier but it was never enough for me and I just kept pushing my luck until, once again, the only winner was the bookies.

By four o'clock that afternoon all my money had gone. I'd completely blown it and there was no going back to the bank so the only other place to go was the pub. "What a f***ing load of s**t!" I screamed through clenched teeth as I kicked the door leaving the bookies.

I'd got a few quid left and thought I'd try and drown my sorrows, it was the only way I knew to try and cope with the instant depression that always followed losing. London was a lonely place when you were skint and I felt like crap. Staring into the bottom of a glass wasn't going to help but it was the only place I could lose myself.

"Is this s**t ever gonna end?" I wondered. My life had always been like this I never thought I would escape the strong hold drink, drugs and gambling had on me. This was who I was and that was that.

Some people were academic, some were sensible and reliable (and boring I thought) and then there were people like me. People who lived on the edge and were never satisfied. People who had a void inside, and no matter what they put into it, it would never be full. It may be full for a day or even a week but that aching would always come back to haunt them.

It was mentally and sometimes physically painful but for some reason I would never give up searching for the answer to life's questions and at that moment in time, I was looking for them in the bottom of a bottle, in the high I got from cocaine or from the thrill of the chase in the bookies.

9
Del boy

My time at RADA was short. The course itself was three years long but I only lasted a year. You could see by my life style that my addictions were merely outward signs of inner turmoil. My drinking had become more and more intrusive. Some times I'd miss classes and even disappear from college for days at a time because I'd be out drinking or gambling. This didn't go unnoticed by the principal. He told me how much he knew saying just before I was asked to leave. "In all the years I've been working here you have been in my office more times than anyone else and for all the wrong reasons." It was time to go, I had blown all the money available to me and when my sponsors caught on to the fact that I'd abused my funding they withdrew from any further involvement. I'd cocked it up yet again just like my Aunt and Mum had predicted.

I had nowhere to go and vowed to all at RADA that this wouldn't be the last they saw of me, "I will make it big," I proclaimed optimistically, although I wasn't sure that I believed it myself anymore.

I borrowed some money from a fellow student and made my way back to Loughborough managing to stay at a friend's house temporarily.

I was homeless again and had no idea how I was going to pick myself back up this time. It seemed I had fallen further than ever before. I got in touch with an old mate of mine who was the local supplier of all things dodgy and he let me have some stuff on tick (Have now, pay later) enabling me to start selling copy designer clothes and accessories around town.

I'd done this type of work on and off for years when in Loughborough and could earn quite good money at it, especially when the students were in town. It was most lucrative around September when they were starting their respective courses and would have just received their grants. All students spend, spend, spend during the first few weeks, getting drunk round town and acting like they were loaded, making themselves easy targets to sell to. I'd wait for them by Barclays Bank in the Market Square and when they were at the cash machine I would appear with a huge bag over my shoulder full of very well made copies of 'Ralph Lauren' shirts and 'Stone Island' jumpers etc. a bit like Del Boy.

"Here mate," I'd say, "I've got a load of knocked off gear going cheap, you want some?" half opening the bag so they could see my wares. "Yeah ok, let's have a look," they'd say, easily reeled in within seconds and once I had got the gear out I was guaranteed to make a sale. I wasn't the only one selling in town but you could bet your bottom dollar I would sell more than anyone else getting nearly double the amount for each item compared to the competition.

I'd become well known round town for being a bit of a 'Jack the lad' and had a bit of a reputation as I was always selling something dodgy. At the height of my selling a few years earlier, I was making about four hundred quid a week. I must have been stealing loads of business from the shops in town and started to build up a large group of regular customers. I also became known for my heavy drinking and flamboyant gambling habit, which ultimately would be my undoing. Other than that I didn't have a care in the world, I just didn't give a s**t and never took anything seriously, so when it came to paying bills and the like I gave them a wide berth. I had outstanding debts with people all over town, rent arrears with the council and countless court fines I'd not paid as a result of theft, GBH and ABH. There was a warrant out for my arrest and I had debt collectors knocking on my door at least twice every week.

I suppose it was only a matter of time before they caught up with me. I'd been in court many times before, firstly getting warnings for fighting and theft then as I kept reappearing, the warnings turned to fines and finally threats of imprisonment.

I wasn't scared of prison, or so I thought, until one Friday on the way to the bookies in town, a police car pulled up next to me. Two coppers jumped out and told me to stop. They were the usual type, outwardly clean cut but probably as corrupt as I was on the inside. One was about six-foot and he did all the talking, the other was much smaller and seemed to cower behind the taller guy. Both had short dark hair and facially looked quite similar. All coppers looked the same to me; I was probably blinded by the uniform. They walked over looking at me suspiciously and asked me were I had come from and where I was going. I told them I had come from home and was going to the betting shop. They didn't believe me and said, "We have reason to believe you may be involved with a house burglary down Nottingham Road and based on our suspicions we are going to search you."

"No you're not!" I protested "I've done nothing wrong; you've no right to search me."

"Listen mate," he said, "you fit the description of the guy we are looking for and if you don't let me search you I'll have to arrest you on suspicion of burglary, do you understand? Now, if you're innocent you have nothing to worry about, have you?"

I shook my head in defiance. "I don't believe this," I replied, "go on then," I said holding my hands up. They carried out the search there on the street. Passers-by were looking at me. In their eyes I had already been branded a criminal which p***ed me off. I was, but they didn't know that.

The old bill didn't find anything on me. I actually was innocent of those particular accusations and when they had taken my name and address they drove off leaving me by the road.

I was quite near the bookies at the time and as I walked in I saw all the usual faces were there.

"Did you see that?" I said wanting to tell someone of the injustice that had just been served and to slag off the police.

"See what?" some one shouted.

"Those f**king coppers," I grunted but I had opened my mouth too soon and at that very moment the same police officers pulled up outside.

"Hey Johnny, they must fancy you!" someone shouted from across the room.

"What the f**k do they want now?" I said. They walked in and the place went quiet.

"Jonathan Kinch?" said the tall one like he had never seen me before.

"Yes, what do you want now?" I replied in a patronising voice.

"Just to let you know that we are no longer holding you under suspicion of the burglary down Nottingham Road. However when I entered your details into our computer it showed that there is a warrant out for your arrest for non-payment of fines, blah, blah, blah. You don't have to say anything…" etc, etc, etc.

I was carted out of the bookies swearing and shouting and bundled into their car whilst all the punters in the bookies looked on in silence. Just my bloody luck! I was driven off shaking my head and looking out the window. I went through all the usual procedures at the nick, emptying my pockets, taking my belt off and shoe laces out, giving my finger prints etc. After being held a number of hours in a small, cold police cell, I was let out on bail and told to appear in court the following Monday.

Boy did I get drunk that weekend! Just in case it was my last chance for a while you understand. Different people were trying to wind me up saying I was going down but I thought I could talk my way out of it and maybe get away with a reduced fine as some of the fines were more than three years old. Maybe they would just drop them altogether because I was on the dole and out of work. I was told that if I was skint they might lower my repayments especially if I promised to be a good lad. Well that was my plan and my solicitor seemed to think the same thing, so when Monday morning came round I woke up feeling quite optimistic about the outcome.

I got up thinking "I won't be there long" so just threw on my tracksuit bottoms and a sweater, had some breakfast then casually walked down to the magistrate's court without a care in the world.

10

Straight jacket

Thinking back I was so cocky about it. I strolled in there begrudgingly just wanting to get out as quickly as possible. I checked in at the main desk and the receptionist told me I was down to see the Judge at 10.30 am. It was now 10.15 so I went outside for a cigarette and coffee. I wasn't nervous at all; in fact I was certain I was going home that morning with just a slap on the wrist and a ticking off. I finished my fag and went in and sat down. The usher came out, clipboard in hand, and was scanning up and down with her finger whilst looking over the top of a pair of half moon glasses "Jonathan Kinch," she called looking in my direction. I nodded my head letting her know it was me, got up and followed her into court where I was told to sit down.

The judges were still in there from the previous cases. I was never any good at paying bills but thought it wasn't really going to matter. I was simply going to persuade the Judge I was a reformed character and would start paying from now on.

I was called to the dock. "I swear to tell the truth, the whole truth and nothing but the truth, so help me God," I declared but it meant absolutely nothing to me at the time. "Are you Jonathan Kinch of blah, blah, blah?" asked the prosecutor "Yes that's correct," I replied. He then continued to read out the charges. I was quite surprised with the length of my record. I sounded like a real hardened criminal when they reeled off all the fines, which were the results of numerous previous assaults. They were all committed under the influence of alcohol or to do with feeding one of my many addictions. There was ABH, GBH, theft, common assault and I was guilty of all the charges. There was no doubt about that but I had managed to dodge the fines for years.

The prosecution then went on to explain, to the Judge, the whole situation. The fact that I had evaded the police for some time now and that it was only by chance that they stumbled across me.

"So, Mr Kinch, why haven't you paid your fines before now?" demanded the Judge. I fed him some cock and bull story about having serious mental health problems (which I didn't think I had at the time) and that I was on the dole and didn't have any money.

"Nothing seems to go my way," I said. He just stared at me, knowing full well that I was telling a pack of lies. It wasn't the first time he would have heard that crock of s**t and he was having none of it.

"So how are you going to pay off these fines now then Mr Kinch?" he asked.

"I don't know. Can't you just scrap 'em?" I said nonchalantly.

"No I cannot!" snapped the Judge. "Mmm," he said as he pondered his next move like he was playing a game of chess. He looked like a right snotty t**t with his little glasses and grey comb over. "Well you clearly have no money so what do you suggest I do with you Mr Kinch?" he asked.

"I don't know, send me down," I said sarcastically.

"Right then, that's what we'll do," he said without hesitation "What's the maximum we can give him for this offence?" he asked the solicitor with his nose stuck up in the air.

"Twenty one days," came the reply.

"Fine. Twenty one days it is then, send him down," ordered the judge. I couldn't believe it! What the f**k did I say that for?

"All stand," said the usher as the Judge got up and left.

I was told to sit down again and wait. Then to my surprise everyone left for lunch. I was just left there sat at the back of the court on my own. What on earth was going on? This is surreal. I started thinking about doing a runner but then thought about the sentence that I would get when they finally caught up with me again and I didn't fancy that so I stayed put.

I waited and waited and waited and then finally an hour later a small stocky guy in a Group 4 security uniform turned up and asked me if I was the chap he was looking for. I told him I was and had been waiting there for ages. "I could have done a runner," I said.

With that he walked me outside to the (Sweatbox) prison van and in I went. It was minging! Inside was a narrow corridor with four caged compartments on each side. I was bundled into one near the back on the right hand side. There was a window in my compartment and from the outside it looked like a normal sized van window but from the inside you could only see out of a small portion of it and then only when standing on tip toes. To be honest it was more like a standing coffin both in shape and size. I didn't like it at all.

After waiting for about ten minutes, while they loaded a couple of other guys in, we set off and before long we were on the motorway heading north. I strained to look out of the window so I could get an idea where we were and saw a sign for Manchester. "F**king hell," I said "What we going up there for?" I sat back thinking what a t**t I'd been over the past few years and started going over all the things I had f**ked up that had led me into the situation I was in.

What was going to happen to me now? What was I going to do without my medication? Would I lose my accommodation?

"I can't f**king handle this!" I thought slamming my head in my hands and letting out a long weary sigh. I was on the verge of breaking down; I could feel my emotions quite literally just under my skin. "I can't let anyone see me like this or I'll be dead meat" I told myself with urgency, trying desperately to reassure myself. I had to keep it together, I had to be strong but I felt like I could lose it at any minute.

We pulled up outside Manchester Prison to drop of some inmates and were let out for a cigarette. It felt like I had been in there for days already. My nostrils sucked in the fresh air and fear gripped me. I was already stressed out just from being in the van what the f**k was I gonna be like cooped up in a cell with God knows who. "Don't be long," said the screw (prison officer). "We aren't staying, you lot are going to Welford Road Prison, Leicester."

"I don't believe this s**t" I thought, it was stuff like this that would send me over the edge. I would get so stressed out at the thought of being trapped with no way out. It was bad enough being inside this box, how would I handle a cell? I was extremely quiet for the rest of the journey afraid of what was going to happen and kept going over different scenarios one by one.

When we arrived I was a nervous wreck. "Come on out you get," said one of the screws.

We had driven into the courtyard of Welford Road Prison through the huge wooden gates that I'd see from time to time when passing through Leicester on the bus. I never thought things would get so bad that I'd ever go in there. How wrong I was.

I was taken into a holding cell and sat there in disbelief as I tried to shrivel into the corner not wanting to be noticed. There were a couple of other people in there who seemed to know each other quite well. They were really loud and didn't seem fazed at all by their surroundings. In fact they seemed pretty much at home and had clearly been in there before. One of them started talking of how he'd been arrested and I heard something about guns. At this point I was feeling really weak and if he'd turned round and shouted "boo!" I would have probably crapped myself; I was in such a fragile state of mind. I was dangerous when I was like that though. I may have felt weak mentally but I was actually really strong physically. Often when I was mentally at my weakest and felt in danger I'd become aggressive but that was always a last resort, unless of course, I was drunk.

The cell door flung open. "Kinch," said the screw beckoning me out with his hands. You could tell he had been there for years by the way he dealt with the inmates. Although he wasn't a big man, in fact he was quite small with wiry, grey hair, he had a confidence about him that made me listen to what he was saying and not question it. "Take your clothes off and put these on," he said, handing me some prison issue clothes.

I didn't like the sound of that but what was I going to do? I gingerly took off my clothes and trying to hide my manhood, put on the grey tracksuit bottoms and top I had been given. "Do you want to keep your trainers on or wear these?" he asked, I took one look at the crappy white plimsolls he was holding and said quietly "Keep mine." He then reeled off a load of stuff to me. I can't remember what it was he said as my senses were overloaded and I felt really strung out. He could have told me I had won the lottery at that point and it would have got the same quiet bewildered response.

"Come on then, this way," he said. I was escorted through a yard and into another building along a landing that was lined with prison cells. There were loads of inmates standing outside their respective cell doors chatting and passing the time. As we went down some metal stairs, I looked up and saw five or six floors of landings above me and then it really hit home that this wasn't just a dream but a horrible nightmare that I might never wake up from. I reached the bottom and was shown to a cell.

"In you go!"

About ten feet from my cell there were a load of lads behind a wire

mesh divider. "Johnny," I heard someone yell. I looked round and recognised a guy I knew called Andy. "Alright mate what you doing here?"
he shouted.

I didn't feel like talking so I just nodded and went inside. The door
slammed behind me and I sat on my bed listening to the keys and chains
rattling as I was locked in.

A shutter opened in the door and the screw that had just brought me
in peered through to see if my cellmate and me were calm. I just stared
back at him then he left.

I had been put in a cell with an Asian guy from Derby who was due
to be released later that week. I can't remember his name but he didn't
seem fazed at all by being in there and casually sat down on his bed like
he had just got in from work or something. He was about five foot eight
and had a little goatee beard. As soon as it went quiet he reached into
his pants and pulled out some weed and rolled a spliff (joint). "Want
some?" he said.

"Why not?" I answered.

Time passed so slowly from then on in and during every second of each
awful hour of the first two days and nights my mind was becoming more
and more unstable. I wasn't sleeping well and got so bored during the
day. I just wasn't used to my own company and spending all this time
practically in solitude was doing my f***ing head in. I hadn't had my
medication, which was Prozac at the time – 200mg a day – the highest
recommended dose. I had been prescribed them for manic depression
and obsessive compulsive disorder (OCD) and when I didn't have them,
I would get withdrawal symptoms like electric shocks running through
my body every time I took a step or moved my eyes.

Having OCD was really s**t. It started out with the odd thought that
I couldn't control and then as they were left to their own devices they
became more and more intrusive. Some of the thoughts would be so evil
and violent that I would become anxious at their presence. This would lead
me to doing drugs and drinking heavily so I could temporarily escape,
blot them out. This in itself was a form of self-medication. I was now in
uncharted water, as I had never been left to deal with what was in my
head without the aid of alcohol and drugs. As well as having intrusive
thoughts, I became obsessive about doing certain things like locking
the door (which wasn't going to be a problem in prison!). When I was
at home I would check the door locks about twelve times before going

to bed. You see twelve was one of my special numbers as was 2, 4, 6, 24 and infinity. Without really knowing it, I would spend hours everyday, counting things around me such as patterns on wallpaper, words on signs or any number of other things. My reasoning was that I had to fit everything into even numbers or something terrible would happen to me. So if I counted only thirteen words on a sign I would make it even by splitting one into two. ½ and ½ add 12 + 12 together and you get 24. (Well it made sense to me at the time!) So, as you can see, my head was full of numbers and all kinds of crap so when I'd been to see the doctor the day before and he said "Oh don't worry you'll be alright," I could have kicked his f***ing head in!

"I wont be alright you t**t," I said.

By now it was tea time and we were called cell by cell for our food, as they didn't want to let too many prisoners out at once in case of trouble.

There was only one toilet in the cell, which was made of metal and positioned in between the beds. There was no dividing wall either to give you privacy, which made things difficult for me because I'm not the kind of guy who would even fart in front of someone never mind take a s**t. So as soon as the other guy left for his grub, I'd quickly jump on the bog and drop the kids off at the pool so to speak (take a dump). It was the only way I could do it without feeling totally humiliated. Then afterwards I'd go upstairs to the canteen where I'd be given a metal tray into which would be dumped a handful of slop they said was food by a guy wearing a blue plastic glove as they didn't use spoons to serve you for some reason. It was minging! I didn't eat after that and completely lost my appetite.

Then we were sent off to our cells where we had to eat because we hadn't been allocated a wing yet. I would flush my food straight down the loo. Even the thought of what might be in there made me feel sick.

It was now the third day and I was in real difficulty. I felt claustrophobic and began experiencing all sorts of ailments.

You see as well as having (OCD) I was a hypochondriac. I'd been in and out of hospital having checks for one thing or another and my mind would latch onto an illness I'd heard about and before long I would be experiencing the symptoms. I believed I was destined to die from something out of the ordinary and would look for ways to confirm that I had a terminal illness. I was convinced I'd got AIDS and in the past two years had been for three separate tests, all of which had confirmed I was negative. Even then I wouldn't be satisfied, convincing myself that they had made a mistake thus, prolonging my own agony.

We were kept in our cells 23 hours of the day until they found a suitable wing for us. By this time I'd had enough and started walking around the cell like a caged animal going out my mind. The other guy who was in there thought I had lost the plot (which I had).

I went over to the cell door and started banging on it "Give me some medication," I shouted. Nothing happened, and then I noticed a button near the door to press in emergencies so I pressed it as hard as I could over and over again. Within minutes a screw appeared and opened the hatch to see what was going on. "What's up?" he snapped. "I need my medication I've not had any since I came in," I shouted.

"Stop moaning you pussy and keep the noise down," he replied then slammed the hatch and left me standing there desperate for help but with no way of getting any. I paced around again mumbling to myself becoming more and more agitated.

"I can't bear it anymore!" I yelled and pressed the buzzer for the second time and with more urgency. Within seconds two screws came running to the door and opened it. They were both big blokes. One had short black hair and the other was bald but both were over six foot two as they towered over me. "What's the matter mate?" the bald guy said in a nice calm tone. "I shouldn't be in here I'm not a criminal and I need my medication. Can I see the doctor?" I pleaded in a subdued strained voice.

"Come on then, come with us and we'll take you to see the doctor," he said. I walked out of the cell with them feeling relieved that someone wanted to help me. They took me down a corridor to a room on the right, opened the door and pushed me inside.

"Take your f**king clothes off now. All of them!" yelled the one with dark hair.

"What! Why?"

"Just do it now!" he demanded. He had some sort of garment in his hand and after I had taken my clothes off and was standing there holding my bits he grabbed my arm and marched me across the corridor into another cell. It was small with no bed, just a piece of wood about the size of a door on the floor where a bed might have been. There was no glass in the window only bars, the light was on and there were some small grey cardboard boxes on the floor, which were to take a dump in.

Apparently they give you those as it helps to do your head in. To have to smell your own crap all day and night reminds you of the s**t urine (ha, ha).

I was pushed through the door and fell to the floor.

"Here," he threw a straight jacket at me.

"Any more noise from you and your going in it!" he said, slamming the door behind him. I didn't say another word and went into shocked panic. I sat there silent for ages, not a thought in my head, it was like my brain had frozen and was trying to reboot. I stayed still, head fixed forward, staring like a rabbit caught in the headlights. My heart was beating like a drum I was so afraid, not so much of the prison though but of my own thoughts. They started coming back again thick and fast. "You're going to lose it completely. You're going to end up in that straight jacket. You're never getting out of here. You're going to end up hurting someone then they will keep you in forever."

I put my head in my hands and cried. It was dark and late in the night; I was cold and scared and sat there trying to keep warm by wrapping the straight jacket around me. I had nothing left in me, I was lost and broken and needed help. In my desperation I cried out to God. "If you are up there please help me. Please get me out of here God and I promise I will try to be a better person and I will never gamble again."

I didn't know if anyone had heard my cry and I just lay there snivelling until somehow I managed to fall asleep.

I didn't dream of anything that night and was abruptly awoken the next morning by the sound of the cell door being noisily opened.

"Breakfast!" The screws must have changed shifts during the night. This was a different guy who seemed much nicer.

"What you doing in here?" he asked. I didn't answer. His face looked kind and he seemed to genuinely care

"Eat up and I'll be back in a bit," he said smiling.

I hungrily ate the food even though it was minging and sat back shivering against the wall. I had no idea what the day would bring and couldn't help thinking, if I wasn't careful, it might be like the previous night's events. The cell door was opened again.

"Here put these on," said the nice screw helping me up and returning my prison clothes. I quickly put them on and stood up.

"Come with me, the Governor wants to see you," he said.

"What now?" I thought. As we walked down the corridor I could hear people shouting and banging and hoped that somehow a miracle might happen and my nightmare would end. I was told to wait outside as the screw went inside an office. I stood there crapping myself like I was gonna be sentenced to death or something. After a few minutes I was called in.

"Kinch," said the Governor; he didn't look like a governor, or what I thought a governor would look like. He was young for a start, in his late forties with short dark hair, and he didn't have a posh accent like the stereotypical ones you see in TV shows like Porridge.

"I've had a look at your record and it says you have been to RADA and that you're in here for non payment of fines", he said.

"That's right," I said wondering where he was going with this.

"You shouldn't be in here lad. You've got yourself in a right mess haven't you?" he said whilst sifting through a few papers. "Well it's your lucky day lad. I'm going to give you a phone card and if you can get someone to pay the rest of your fine, I'm going to let you out."

"Really?" I was stunned.

"Yes, really!" he replied.

No one knew I was in prison but if I contacted someone surely they would understand my predicament and help me out.

He gave me a card and I was shown to the phone although I didn't know who the hell I was I going to call. Paul Sharp was a mate of mine who had always bailed me out in the past. Thankfully I have a pretty good memory and knew his mobile number. It rang for ages then eventually he picked up. I told him where I was and explained the situation but he couldn't help me even though I begged. B*****s!

I didn't know who else to call and out of desperation I called my older brother Jason.

I had been in the s**t many times before and Jason had had to bail me out, so I wasn't too sure if he would do the same again this time. I had no other choice. I had to swallow my pride and call him.

The phone was ringing and as soon as he answered it I burst into a tirade of emotion filled banter, begging him to help me out and vowing to pay him back as soon as possible. To my relief and surprise he agreed. I told him the amount and where to come and he said he would do it straight away. I will never forget his kindness that day, thank you Jay!

I put the phone down with mixed emotions. My brother was a hero, I couldn't believe I was going to get out of here, it was fantastic yet I was still hurting and confused and felt mentally damaged from the experience. I went back and told the Governor the result of my phone call and he seemed genuinely pleased for me.

"Make sure you don't find yourself back in here again."

"Don't worry, I won't," I said, thanking him. I was taken back to my cell to wait until my brother arrived.

The time seemed to go slowly whilst I waited for him. All I could think about was what I was going to do when I got out. One thing was for sure; I would never gamble again. I remembered a phrase I had once heard and I kept going over it again and again in my mind. "Prison walls and prison bars do not make a prison; it's what's inside a man's mind."

These words rang true to me as I was already in prison in my own head even before I was banged up, and being in Welford Road nick just magnified and intensified the chaos inside me.

It was about 11 am and I heard the now familiar sound of keys and a chain jangling in the lock of my cell door. It swung open.

"Come on Kinch you've been given a reprieve."The screw said. I jumped up off the bed faster than Linford Christie coming out the starting blocks. We left the cell and walked up the same stairs I'd walked down four days before. Inmates stood around looking on, menacing and envious of my release. "Good f***ing riddance," I thought as they glared at me as if I had two heads. We went out through an exercise yard and into the building where I'd been previously issued my prison clothes. I took them off and put my own clothes back on, signed some paper work and then was led out into the yard. I breathed in the fresh air and closed my eyes for a split second. I was almost there; the only thing that separated me from the outside world was a huge set of wooden doors. A prison guard checked my papers and opened a small door framed within one of the big doors and released me. My brother was waiting outside with his car and greeted me with a hug.

Things were not the same anymore; everything looked different to me somehow. It felt like I had been in there for years and even though I was free on the outside, on the inside I was still in chains.

As we pulled off and I looked back at what had been my lowest point so far, I thought to myself more seriously than ever before "What is going to become of you Johnny Kinch?"

11

A moment of sobriety

I returned to the hostel feeling really depressed and in need of a drink after losing on the horses yet again. I managed to cadge a few cans of beer off different guys who owed me favours and went and sat across the road from the hostel on the triangle with a couple of the alkies who I had become quite good mates with. The Triangle was the nickname of a small island in the middle of all the traffic, right outside Shaftsbury Avenue theatre, where you could sit and get totally out your face and not be bothered by the old bill. And as the night went by we drank more and more, becoming increasingly lairy towards any passers by who so much as glanced at us. I can't remember too much about what happened next as I was out of it but I'll give you an idea. Two smartly dressed guys carrying small rucksacks were coming our way, you could tell they were tourists. I asked them for a cigarette and got no answer so I shouted out again.

"Give us a fag mate." One of them looked round and said something which sounded like "F**k off" to me so, fuelled by alcohol and seeing red I ran over to them grabbing one by the jacket. He looked at me with fear and started saying stuff really fast in a foreign language.

"What the f**k you on about?" I screamed at him. I didn't give a s**t at the time and started yanking his arm and yelled at him to give me his money. He couldn't understand what I was saying so I made gestures to him with my eyes, which must have looked like those of a mad man. My rational thoughts of "What are you doing?" were drowned out by the drink and rage and then I really lost the plot and started throwing him around like a wet rag until he eventually realised what I wanted and took out his wallet dropping it on the floor. I stopped yanking him around, letting go of him long enough so I could pick it up. As soon as

I'd released my grip he ran off down the road as fast as he could with his mate following behind him.

My heart was racing. All I could think was "S**t, I'd better get out of here" and started running heading towards Soho.

"What the f**k have you done now Johnny Kinch?" I asked myself through gritted teeth and with eyes as wide as saucers. As I looked at the wallet in my hand I had a moment of sobriety, realising that what had just happened was real and definitely not good.

I made my way to an all night café and as I walked in it felt like everyone knew what I had just done. I couldn't look anyone in the face and ordered a coffee without making eye contact with the guy behind the counter. I felt as guilty as sin and gingerly sat down trying to blend in with the crowd. I definitely couldn't go back to the hostel yet; the incident had taken place too near it for comfort.

I stayed there anxious and fidgeting until the early hours of the morning, and only when I had sobered up I made my way back to the hostel. There was nobody on the streets by that time and I let out a sigh of relief, keeping my head down until I'd gone into the hostel unseen. Thankfully there was nobody in my room that night so I got straight into bed. I knew what I had done was wrong but it was too late now. I could still see his face and hear the yelling in my head. "Piss off!" I told my own thoughts, shutting my eyes tightly trying to force myself to sleep, hoping that this nightmare would go away forever. I managed to drop off and stayed in bed until mid morning but I was still wrestling with my guilty conscience. I couldn't lie there any longer and had to get up no matter how guilty I felt about it. Besides, I had money now and started thinking about what I was going to do with it.

I looked in the wallet and found a load of notes. "Nice one," I muttered but there was only one problem they were all foreign. I had a quick think about it and my desire to gamble was so strong that I decided I would go to a bank and change the money into English, even though it was a bit risky. I had to be careful though I couldn't get caught red handed. Even though I had committed a heinous crime there was no way I could even consider admitting that I was in the wrong and so I tried to justify it in my own mind by passing it off as a mistake and looked for blame in the victim instead. After all, if they hadn't of told me to f**k off, it would never have happened. I was desperate to believe my own lies.

I got to the bank and handed my loot to the teller and watched nervously while she counted it.

"Thirty five quid is that all?" I said with my heart sinking. I let out a huge sigh and inside began complaining to myself, "I did all that for just thirty five lousy quid! What a t**t!" Well there was only one thing for it so I headed off to the bookies to try and double my dough. It was way too early for normal racing but as any addicted gambler will tell you it's never too early for virtual racing.

Virtual racing was basically animated horses or dogs racing around a computer generated track. You didn't stand a chance of winning; it really was daylight robbery. Ironic wasn't it? Although the horses or dogs were nothing more than cartoon they could still fall or get hampered but us suckers still thought we could beat the system.

I passed by an off licence on the way and bought some fags and a couple of cans. To be honest, I didn't feel too good handing over dirty money, I even felt like the shop keeper knew where it had come from and was looking at me in disgust.

I got to the bookies and not surprisingly within fifteen minutes or so the money was gone. I might as well have just given them the f***ing money on my way in and saved myself a bit of time. My head, heart and everything else sank to the depths of despair. "What a f***ing idiot. What the hell am I going to do now?"

There was so much negativity in my mind I didn't know how much longer I could cope with it. I knew I had to change my life but hadn't the faintest idea how? I felt completely trapped and believed 100% that no matter how hard I tried I would never be able to stop the vicious circle of gambling, drinking and doing drugs. I had failed at everything in the past and somehow always managed to destroy any glimmer of hope for a future. I wandered off into town. Walking around Covent Garden watching rich people having fun whilst I was skint and deeply depressed can't have done me any good. I couldn't remember the rest of that day or just didn't want to.

12

Drained

My room-mate Tommy came in at about 3.30 am very loud and off his head.

"Will you shut up, I'm trying to sleep!" I shouted at him. He didn't respond and lay down on his bed smoking a fag. The room went quiet again and I fell asleep. I was dreaming again, then suddenly, Bang! "What the f**k!" Something had hit me on the head, bounced off and hit the floor. He had thrown his alarm clock at me and it was now happily ringing away by itself. I could see Tommy sat up on his bed, though not very well as I was half-asleep "What you do that for?" I yelled as I sat up holding my head and rubbing my eyes. As my eyes started to clear I got a glimpse of what I thought was blood, I squished my eyes together and blinked a couple of times trying to clear my vision and looked again.

It was blood alright, it was running down his hands and collecting in a pool on the floor "What have you done you t**t?" I said, getting out of bed and moving over towards him. He'd cut his wrists with a piece of broken glass but not in the usual way from side to side, he'd torn open the veins down his arms exposing them length ways. He looked drained and pale. His wrists looked a right mess "Oh you idiot what have you done?" I said grabbing a towel to stem the flow of blood. "Keep pressure on it I'll go down and get staff." I had to run down eight flights of stairs half-asleep and not quite believing what was happening. When I got there completely out of breath I told staff the situation. They were night workers; most of them foreign from Ghana and didn't speak much English. They looked at me like I was scum and didn't want to know. "Come on it's serious call an ambulance!" I screamed at them, but they didn't even flinch, not paying the slightest bit of attention to my pleas for help, as if I didn't even exist. I ran back up the stairs to the room as

59

fast as I could. "I've got to pack up smoking," I thought as I coughed my lungs up towards the top. I burst into the room half expecting him to be dead. He had collapsed onto the floor. I started slapping him around the face shouting his name "Tommy." By passing out he had taken the pressure off his wounds and blood was now flowing freely from them, although it was slower than before. I'd learnt some first aid whilst in the Marines and managed to stop the bleeding temporarily. "Come on get up," I shouted, lifting him to his feet and somehow managing to get him into the lift and downstairs.

He was extremely drunk and had taken a load of Diazepam, which thankfully had slowed his heart rate down enough to staunch the flow of blood, probably saving his life. We had to get a taxi to the hospital, as the staff were still reluctant to assist even after seeing him. It was a long night sitting with him in the hospital, he had tried to refuse any sort of assistance at first but I managed to persuade him and finally he got treated.

His wrists were sown up and bandaged, then we went back to the hostel and I put him to bed. I don't think he even knew what was going on and as soon as his head hit the pillow he was out cold, sleeping like a baby. Why does this s**t happen to me?

I lay there in bed, thinking about the sequence of events over the past few days. I didn't know whether I was coming or going. One minute I'm mugging someone, threatening to kill them, then the next I'm saving someone. It certainly felt better helping than hurting but even though I really wanted to do good, I couldn't for doing bad.

I wasn't sure if I could sleep after all that. What if Tommy got up in the night and stabbed me?

I tried to stay awake as long as possible but my tired mind and body got the better of me and I drifted off around five o'clock.

13

Eastenders

I'd been in the hostel a couple of months by now and had become quite well known around the West End by some of the doormen and a few of the regular drinkers. I was never happy slumming it and on the odd occasion when I won a few quid I'd go and buy a load of clothes then hit the town with a bit of coke.

The nice clothes didn't last long though. When I ran out of money again I would clean them up, pick the stitching and take them back to the shop claiming they were faulty to get my money back. Even if I lost the receipt it didn't matter. I had become an expert at arguing with shop managers for a refund. Many would refuse at first but I would just keep on and on getting louder and louder making a right spectacle of myself until they gave in and refunded me the full amount just to get me out the shop. This would happen almost on a daily basis. "If some of these shops employed me I could save them a fortune" I thought. I knew every angle and every trick in the book because I had used them all. I wrote the book!

When I was out on the town I might go to the Comedy Store, the Voodoo Lounge and some of the bars in Leicester Square. Nobody knew I lived in a hostel and why would I tell them? Everyone was so image and money orientated in London nobody would have given me a second glance if they knew my circumstances.

One night I decided to go looking for a job and went out as dressed up as possible. I asked around a few bars and clubs and wasn't having much joy so I decided to go to the Voodoo Lounge for a drink. It's a really cool place where loads of rich and famous people go. Inside were a number of rooms. The Cigar lounge was where the so-called "gents" could hang out and talk business. Then there was the Flame bar which was decorated in what looked like reddish turtle shell all over the walls and down the side of the bar, which was lit from behind giving the impression of flames everywhere. The bling bling didn't stop there either, when you went to the bogs you would be met by a great big chap from Nigeria who would give you a quick spray of any of the aftershave you could see on the shelf, and believe me there were loads. I'd never seen anything like it. To top it all off, there was a picture of the queen on the wall watching over you while you siphoned the python (that's take a pee to you and me). I ended up hanging around by the main entrance and got chatting to one of the guys on the door who turned out to be the manager. His name was Dan and funnily enough he was originally from Leicester, he seemed a really nice chap and easy to talk to. He was about twenty-five years old, six foot tall and of medium build. I struck up a conversation with him about some of the clubs he had worked at and he said he had heard of my brother JFK. "Wow," I thought, "this is a perfect chance to get some work." I asked him if there were any jobs going there and he told me they did have a vacancy.

He gave me an application form and asked me to bring it back the next day for an interview. "Nice chatting to you", I said as I walked up the stairs to get the free drink I had talked him into giving me. I was well pleased that he knew my brother. That's probably what got me the job opportunity (Thanks again Jay!)

I had a great time that night and hoped I would end up working there. The next day the interview went well and by the end of it I had a job working as a greeter on the door. A top job, in a top place, as they only have a greeter on the door at the posher more exclusive venues you see.

I had to wear a jacket that looked like one of the collarless suits the Beetles wore in the sixties but who cared? It was just the job for me. It was brilliant. I would be meeting new people and mixing with the rich and famous, what more could I ask for? I knew I would make the most of such an opportunity and before long it looked like I had.

One night on shift a familiar face walked in. It was Sean Maguire, a young looking Irish actor, who was in Eastenders. He came up to the desk and asked if a Mr Simon Darwell Taylor had been in yet.

"Sorry, not that I know of," I said.

"Well, could you tell him Sean is upstairs in the Flame bar?" he asked in a very soft southern Irish accent.

"Of course, no problem mate," I replied. "What does he look like?"

He gave me a description and told me he was there to meet him about a film they were making then off he went. "Well f**k me, Sean Maguire," I thought. Ever the opportunist, my mind started working overtime. If I played my cards right I may get some work out of this. About an hour later in walked a chap I thought could be Mr Darwell-Taylor. He fitted the description Sean gave me, short, very smartly dressed and going slightly bald. As I was checking him out he started going upstairs so I called out to him.

"Mr Taylor?"

"Yes," he replied.

"Hi, I'm Johnny. I hope this doesn't sound rude but I've seen you before. Aren't you a director?" It was a long shot and cheeky but what had I got to lose?

"Yes, that's right. Do I know you?" he replied.

"No," I said. "I'm an ex RADA student looking for acting work. Sean Maguire told me you were coming to meet him. He's upstairs in the Flame bar waiting for you."

"Oh thanks," he said. "Did you really go to RADA?" he asked.

"Yep and I am looking for acting work, have you got anything going?" I said half jesting. He stopped in his tracks and paused for a moment.

"Actually I might have. What time do you finish?" he asked.

"As it happens in about half an hour," I said.

"Fine come up and see me in the bar when you're done and we can have a chat."

I couldn't believe it. "Will do," I excitedly called back.

I quickly got through the things I was doing and joined them in the bar upstairs. We got on pretty well and they seemed really down to earth. They had been making a film, the majority of which had already been shot and were discussing some final details, one of which being that they didn't yet have anyone to play the part of the murderer that eventually kills off Sean's character. It wasn't a big role and the actor involved would only have a couple of lines but it was perfect for me. After a long discussion between Sean and Simon while I sat at the bar, they called me over and decided they'd take a chance and let me have a go. "Come on!" I yelled "I won't let you down," I told them. It didn't seem real though. I was living in a hostel with all my problems and at the same time I was going to be in a movie with a real speaking part. Even though it was only small I couldn't have cared less. For me this was the shape of things to come. It gave me the lift I really needed and inside I was screaming "The only way is up!", well I hoped.

A few days later I received a call from one of the production team telling me where and when I would be picked up and informing me there would be a script in the post once they had my address. Later that week the script arrived and I was thrilled to bits even though I only had about three lines to say. "Better than f**k all."

The film was called 'Out of Depth'. It was the true story of a guy called Paul Nixon who had got involved with the wrong people in London and had subsequently been murdered. Sean Maguire was playing the lead role (Paul Nixon) and my character appeared right at the end of the film when Sean's character was in prison. I was so excited about it and told everyone I knew I was going to be in a film. I felt like this time, maybe, my big break had come.

On the morning of the shoot, I was picked up at about 5 am from the corner of Neal Street just across the road from the hostel. Some of the crew were already in the car when it arrived for me and everyone seemed really excited about filming. We got chatting and they were all very nice. They had no idea I lived in a hostel and were treating me like a proper actor so I didn't want to say anything or look too overwhelmed by what was going on.

We arrived at about 6am and I was taken onto the set where I was given tea, a full breakfast and everything I wanted. It was great. I loved all the attention and settled in very quickly. "This is the life for me," I thought.

We were filming in the changing rooms of an athletic stadium owned by Linford Christie. It was perfect for what they wanted, poorly lit and very sinister. All the walls were solid concrete and I had to creep up from behind one of them to Sean's character while he was having a wash in a small sink. He was supposedly in the shower rooms of a prison and I had to confront him, have a bit of dialogue, then stab him to death with a sharpened spoon and that's how the film ended. We did numerous rehearsals and then around lunchtime we stopped for a break. During the break, Linford turned up to nosy around and see how we were getting on. He seemed a really nice guy. Very tall and looked every bit as muscular as he does on TV. He came and said hello to Sean and me who were sharing the same dressing room. I didn't say much but Sean being the seasoned professional went off chatting with him. After lunch we got on with it and all went well. The stabbing looked convincing and after it had been checked and re-checked with the director we were told it was a wrap.

It was time to go and I was sad that it had finished to tell the truth. I felt I belonged there on set with other actors, doing what I thought I did best. We all went our separate ways, me to the station to catch the tube and everyone else in their flash cars to go back to their luxury homes and their happy lives. Me, well, my bit of stardom was over for now and the next time I would see them would be at the cast party. I was hoping I could do some networking there and make some contacts. There were surely going to be other actors there and with my wit and charm anything could happen. Maybe if I made a good impression I could have a flash car and a good life too!

The cast party was at 'Bar Denim', bang opposite Stringfellows in the West End. There was a huge queue outside on the night and as I was a cast member I went straight to the front and got in with no problems. "Well, here we go," I thought letting out a long breath and walking to the bar. All I had was twelve quid and I knew it was going to be a struggle to maintain the façade that I was "one of them" with that kind of money.

There were loads of people there and by chatting to as many as possible I could increase my chances of being offered a drink or a line of coke and if I got on with someone really well, I may be able to use the old line "The b***dy cash machine has just eaten my card! Don't suppose you can lend me twenty quid could you?"

You see that because I was cheeky and looked the part, I would normally get a result.

That night I was having a blast. People were giving me Charlie (cocaine) left, right and centre and I was never without a drink. At one point I was chatting to Clive Owen, now a big Hollywood actor. At the time he was in the program Chancer that was airing on TV. I don't know what he was doing there but he was a really nice chap and it's good to see him doing so well now! I didn't get any contacts from him though or anyone else that night and when the film was released it didn't do any good either. It went to the Cannes film festival but to no avail and didn't even make it to the cinema. The best it could do was go straight to video. I remember some years later getting it out from Blockbuster just to see what it was like and to be honest it was a bit disappointing. My hopes of being thrust into stardom were put on hold again but I wouldn't let go of the dream for long. "If I could get a small part in a film whilst living in a hostel, what could I do when my life was back on track?" I thought trying to encourage myself.

The night ended and everyone left, some went on to more intimate, exclusive parties whilst others simply went home. But me, I just walked round the corner to the hostel. It was ironic but I was probably the only one there that night who had long term accommodation in the centre of London, the most expensive place to live in the UK. The only problem was though, it was a hostel, and you could only get a room there if you had a serious drug or drink problem and weren't wanted anywhere else. Very different to the exclusive Hotels in the same area where you could only get a room if you had the right type of credit card and looked the part. The difference between first class and baggage! A bit like my life at the time. One minute I'm mixing with the stars the next minute I'm bedding down with scum in the gutter staring at them. How odd life can be!

14

Sleight of hand

I kept my job at the Voodoo Lounge for the rest of my stay at the hostel then left when I finally got offered a flat in Hackney. It was a nice place, brand new. I was the first person in there so I took it and with the help of a community care grant I moved in. This was great for me, a new start. Surely a change of address would bring a change of circumstances.

The flat had a living room, bedroom and bathroom with fridge and cooker all in; it was just what I had hoped for. Even though this seemed the perfect place I found it quite difficult to settle in. It wasn't that I missed the hostel, I just didn't like being left alone with the nasty thoughts in my head. At least being around others, no matter how low they were, was in some way comforting.

After being there about two weeks I'd gone through all the money I'd got from my grant. I spent some on furniture and the rest on booze and gambling. Now there was nothing left. One restless day, bored out of my brain and desperate for a drink, I sold the furniture and went out and blew that money as well. It was quite rough there and on the first night I heard gun shots. The next day it was on the news that there had been gang warfare at a club round the corner. This put me back on edge and I decided to look for a job to keep me occupied. I had been getting 'The Stage' newspaper (for performing Arts) on a Wednesday so that I could look for auditions.

That particular week there was a job going in Hamley's toy store on Regent Street in the City. It was working for a company called Marvin's Magic and they were looking for someone experienced in performing magic tricks to work in their section of the store demonstrating to thousands of people each day.

Well, I had always loved magic and I knew a few sleight of hand tricks that I had developed myself over the years just to entertain people in the pubs when I was p**sed. Besides, I thought I would pick it up quick enough if I could only blag my way into getting the job.

I called them up and had a chat. They seemed keen and wanted to meet me at Hamley's, so a few days later I went along for an interview/audition.

Hamley's is chaotic to say the least and when I got in there I couldn't believe how many toys and people there were. I made my way down an escalator to the café where I'd been told I was to meet the manager.

"Hi," he said in a South African accent. "Have a seat." We sat down and talked about the job and the interview part was going well at first, he seemed to like me, and I became more and more confident.

I started telling him how good I was but when it came time to show him my tricks I completely blew it. My hands were all over the shop and the coins I was using were flying all over the place. I was getting redder by the second. It didn't seem to bother him though. "Sorry," I said embarrassed.

"Don't worry," he said. "I've seen all I need to see. Johnny you seem like a nice guy. I'll be in touch." We shook hands and I left feeling a little deflated thinking he had fobbed me off.

I caught the number 38 bus back to Hackney from Oxford Street practicing my tricks all the way home and, even though I was on a moving bus I got them right every time, F***ing typical I should have done my audition on the bus!

My phone started ringing just as I was getting off. "Hello," I answered; it was the guy from Marvin's Magic and they wanted to give me the job starting the following Monday.

"Well what do you think?" he said.

"That's fantastic news I'd love the job, thank you," I replied. He went on to tell me that the first week would be learning all the tricks as I would be performing them live in the shop the following week and I needed to be good if I wanted to make any commission. I was excited again at another new phase in my life. Maybe this could be my way out. I had cashed in my income support on the Thursday and it was now Friday, so to celebrate, I went out on the pop.

I awoke around noon the next day with a banging hangover. Something I had done many, many times before. There never seemed any way of getting relief from it. The postman came and I received a T-shirt from

Hamley's with a letter welcoming me to the team and asking me to wear it on my first day. I just grunted and threw it on floor. I was feeling so rough I didn't care and sitting around on my own in the flat was doing my head in so I went to the bookies. I knew it was a bad idea just as I did every time I went there but I just couldn't stop myself. I didn't intend on losing but just in case I left a tenner at home so that I could get to my new job on Monday.

My head was still pounding as I put my first bet on and the fact that my horse won didn't make me feel any better. Then the second and third came in as well, I couldn't believe it. I don't know why I didn't just walk out when I was in front. I wish I had but I couldn't do it, that's what gambling does to you. I just kept on going until all my money was gone and in a weird sort of way, when I'd blown my wad I felt strangely re-lieved. It was as if I thrived not on the winning but the chase. By 3 pm I had given all my money over to the bookies. They had triumphed once again, no surprise there. Was I ever going to have any luck? Then I remembered the money I had left at home. If only I could win back what I came in with I'd be happy at that. I ran to get the money and was back in time for the next race.

I started betting small. I couldn't blow this. Pound by pound my bus fare disappeared until once more I stood there skint in defeat.

In a way I felt almost glad that I had nothing left and could finally go. I slumped off home to my bed and closed my eyes calling myself all the names under the sun and beating myself up for being such a t**t. Why did I keep doing this to myself?

It was as if there were two people living inside me one that destroyed everything and one that was left to pick up the pieces and come up with inventive ways to get me out of the s**t that the first one would always get me in. How on earth was I going to get to work now? I had no money, no food and the bills hadn't been paid since I moved in. Things weren't looking good.

When Monday morning came I got up early went out to the bus stop and jumped on the back of the number 38 going to the West End. It was one of the old red London buses with no doors on the back instead of the new ones with a Perspex screen round the driver at the front. This one had a ticket inspector which gave me a real chance of making it all the way to work without having to pay. I couldn't pay, my failure at the bookies had seen to that. It was a while before the inspector came round for tickets.

"Where you going sir?" asked the short, fat inspector in full uniform and cap. He had quite a nice face so I took a chance.

"Could I have a word with you at the back," I said trying to look embarrassed.

He pulled a funny face but agreed to comply with my request. We walked past the other passengers and reached the recess where the inspector stands.

"Right, this is a rather strange request but as you can see I'm on my way to work," I said, pointing to my T-shirt with Hamley's logo on it. "You see, I've just got this job and today is my first day."

"And?" said the inspector with raised eyebrows.

"Well I've been on the dole for years and well to cut a long story short, I haven't got any money until I get to work and they give me a sub from my wages. I won't do it again," I added quickly.

There was a short pause before the inspector responded "It's your lucky day mate. Go and sit down and make sure you don't do it again," he said. "Hey, and good luck with your job," he shouted.

What a nice bloke. There are some nice people in the world after all. Thinking about it, it wasn't a bad idea to ask for a sub at work either.

I got there ok and my first day went well. I managed to arrange a sub from the company for a couple of hundred quid and yes, you've guessed it. I blew that drinking and gambling too.

This went on the whole time I stayed at Hamley's. I would run out to the bookies in my lunch hour and then when whatever money I had was gone, I would invent more and more elaborate stories to convince my fellow workers to lend me cash. I was getting good at performing magic tricks but even better at tricking my colleagues. But at the time nobody had reason to suspect anything and the boss was so impressed he even talked about me going over to their American store to work there for a while but no matter how talented I was, my addictions were in total control of me and I always bowed to them before anything else.

I was so blind to the fact that I was destroying my life and each time I borrowed I was getting more and more in debt, sealing my fate. With my lifestyle the way it was, it was inevitable that my job would end sooner rather than later.

I started missing work as depression took hold and began hitting the drugs hard again doing whatever I could to earn enough money to feed my habits. In my heart I knew I had just blown another chance to succeed. Another chance of happiness was dead and buried yet I still hoped that, even now, I could pull something out the bag. This would be my greatest trick ever. Changing my life from hell to heaven.

15

Robbie Williams

Throughout this time I'd been jumping the train on regular occasions going back to Leicester to stay at my dad's house. Over time I began to stay in Leicester more than London, so eventually I left the flat in Hackney and moved into a flat down the road from my dad's. It was a flat that a barmaid from the local pub had just moved out of. She had gone to stay at her dad's so she let me stay there for a couple of months. This was an extremely dark time for me. My alcohol usage had increased dramatically and I was now using Diazepam in high doses every day and mixed with drink, it was a lethal cocktail that gave me regular blackouts. I don't remember much about that time, all I know is there was a huge cloud in my head that I just couldn't shake off. I was so down I struggled to find a reason to live each day. At some point in my desperation to break out of my depression, I started going to a bar/club in town that had become very popular called the Lizard Lounge.

I was up to my usual antics doing Magic tricks at the bar and generally being the entertainer. I found it hard to be anything else. Quite sad really, people thought I was so confident and full of life but they had no idea that depression and thoughts of suicide were constantly with me.

I soon became well known for being an entertainer and was getting a lot of requests from people to join them on their tables, so always the clown I would do some tricks and tell some crazy stories. It wasn't long before my antics caught the club owner's eye and I got pally with him and after a few weeks he told me he was looking to put a late night cabaret on in the top room of the Lizard Lounge and asked if would I be interested in coming up with an idea for a night and hosting it. I jumped at the chance; maybe there was a light at the end of the tunnel after all. It was just what I was looking for, my own show. I had been going to quite a few karaoke's over the past few months and had realised I was quite a good singer.

Once I was up there I would joke around on the microphone and get people laughing. I seemed to have a knack at it and people kept telling me I should do my own night.

After thinking about it I went back and told the owner of the club that I wanted to put on a late night comedy karaoke that would be close to the bone and not for the faint hearted. I said I'd be calling my character Kenny Kennedy and would be wearing a seventies suit with a wide collared shirt, wig and glasses. It was easier to control a crowd and you could get away with murder, comedy wise, if you looked more of a t**t than the person you were slagging off.

He loved the idea and I got straight on with putting my act together. I had no idea how it was going to go but had a good feeling that it would work out.

While all this was going on I was still going out on the town enjoying the nightlife doing ever-increasing amounts of coke and getting pissed on a daily basis. In fact, I think I even talked the club owner into giving me wages up front for props etc., but of course I was telling pork pies. The money was going on gambling and drugs as usual.

I was now very good at hiding my gambling problem from those around me. People in the circles I was mixing with did all sorts of bad stuff but being a scummy gambler and always borrowing money was frowned upon. Now coke - that was a different matter, people weren't as bothered about that as it was associated with fun and had a certain social status. Coke was the drug of choice with all the "in people" in town; they were using it regularly but gambling, that was just for low lifes. And you know what? I believed it too. I would deny all involvement with gambling and anyone associated with it when it suited my needs. I was in total denial but I couldn't see it and still thought I could pull myself out of the s**t, hoping this new job might be the answer.

The time came for my debut night at the club and I was really nervous. I had negotiated, as part of my wages, free drinks for the duration of the night and to get some Dutch courage I started on the beer as soon as I got there.

My act started at 10.30pm and finished at about 1.30am. The night involved me as the host and a seemingly normal karaoke. I would sing a load of songs to get everyone in the mood and would take requests as people were filtering in.

I could copy certain people's singing voices and would do Tom Jones, Robbie Williams and sometimes Elton John too. The punters loved it and after great success on the first few nights, word started getting round and anybody who thought they were an entertainer would turn up for the show on a Thursday night. It became so popular that other bar owners started coming down and asked me to perform at their venues on other nights of the week. I negotiated a deal with three other bars and business took off big style.

Things were looking up or so I thought. I was earning a thousand pounds a week but no matter how well I did it was never enough. The more I got the more I spent and the more I needed. I could have set myself up for the future if I'd have had any sense but week in week out the money went up my nose or down the bookies. Things became so bad I stopped paying rent at the flat I had recently moved into and was borrowing more money on the strength of my earnings. I was walking a fine line and hoped and prayed I wouldn't fall off the edge.

One of the places I was now performing was called the Turkey Café. I was doing a Wednesday night and pulling in such crowds that they took on extra staff.

I began a relationship with one of the girls that worked there. I had been in loads of relationships before and each one finished due to my drinking, drug or gambling habit. The odd one ended because I was so suspicious and didn't trust any women. Probably due to the fact that I had cheated on everyone I had ever been with and so thought the same of them.

This relationship was to last longer than the others but the inevitable was going to happen, although not in the way I expected. Her name was Kate. She was blonde and from Cheshire. She was a very driven person and had a good job as a fashion designer, earning a good salary. After only knowing each other for a few weeks and due to the fact I was being evicted from my flat, because I owed them two and a half grand in rent, I moved in with her.

Shortly after moving in, due to my erratic lifestyle my business started going down the pan and after a couple of months I was out of work and on the dole. Things started getting bad between me and Kate and I took financial liberties I shouldn't have. I talked her into lending me money for this and that and because she worked hard and had a good job she would lend me it. It still wasn't enough and over the next few months I began doing less and less until one day Kate came home from work and told me about an advert she had seen in the paper.

16
Soapstars

ITV were auditioning actors to play a new family in Emmerdale. But not only that the whole auditioning and elimination process was to be screened as a series of programmes in their own right. The first auditions had already taken place but they were holding some more at Aston Villa football ground in Birmingham the following week.

At first I thought "No way." I mean, there will be thousands of people there auditioning, what chance would I have? But after thinking about it all weekend I thought, what the heck. Maybe I could do it and make things really change for myself so why not? I deserve it!

Kate took me down to Birmingham early the following Wednesday, hoping to miss the queues. It didn't work. Hundreds of desperate people thought the same thing as we did and when we arrived the queue stretched back as far as we could see.

"F**king hell," I said to Kate.

"Well we're here now so let's join the queue before it gets any bigger," she said. We waited in line for about an hour before Kate started getting fed up and wanted to go home. I told her to stop whining and go, so she gave me the train fare back, as I had zero cash again, and off she went. The queue inched along at a snail's pace for the next five hours before I finally got into the main hall.

Once in there I had to wait another hour but that went really quickly, as I was now being entertained by the countless people with absolutely no talent whatsoever, who were getting turned away in droves. There was one woman who had wrapped herself in bog roll and had come for the part of the mummy. Then there was this girl with copper coloured hair who looked like a right psycho, and when she was rejected she became hysterical and had to be escorted off the premises. It was hilarious!

Others took rejection with ease but most couldn't take it and started crying and causing a scene.

I was getting closer to the front now and started to get a bit nervous myself. What if I got turned away? It was so easy to get caught up in all the excitement, I just hoped I could make it through this first audition then maybe I would be in with a chance.

They weren't really giving you enough time to show them what you could do; some people didn't even open their mouths and were told "No thanks." They were obviously looking for a certain type of person but I didn't have a clue if I was the type they were looking for. The panel was made of two men and one woman. One guy had scruffy grey hair, the other was very well groomed and as camp as a row of tents. The woman had red hair and pale skin with a mean face like the wicked witch of the west. She seemed to be more in control than the other two. It was almost my turn and I was called up onto the side of the stage. I was s**ting myself. Only two more people, then me. "Next," said one of the Judges. I walked on stage confidently and was just about to open my mouth when I heard the woman judge say, "Yes you're through, I like him." I couldn't believe it. I hadn't even said anything. "Come on!" I yelled in excitement thrusting my fist in the air.

I was quickly whisked off for an interview of how I thought it went and who I was, by a film crew that was hanging around trying to get peoples' reactions. I remember telling them my life story in about two minutes flat and saying at the end of it "Maybe this is my year after all!"

Another great chance was put before me. Surely with all of my previous experiences in the hostel, on the streets and at RADA I wasn't going to blow this one. I knew the warning signs and if only I could keep control of my addictions then I would be ok.

The production team stuck a leaflet in my hand to prove I had got through and had been invited for the next audition then gave me a short script from Emmerdale to learn.

I walked off through the crowd like I was royalty and left the building smiling from ear to ear. When the other wanabes that were still queuing outside saw my recall letter they looked at me like I was some kind of celebrity. It was weird but I felt great. I called Kate to let her know the good news then caught the train home dreaming all the way back about what could be.

The second auditions were the next day and that night I had to frantically learn my lines. I'd got a really good memory for learning lines so had no problems memorising scripts but twenty four hours wasn't long. I went back to Villa Park the next day, except this time there was a shorter queue, less competition and we would be working with someone else.

I can't remember who I was paired with but I do know the outcome. After a gruelling day I had made it through again. I was totally exhausted and hadn't realised how stressful auditioning would be and how much it would take out of me. The next set of auditions would be really serious though and I started liking the thoughts I was having about this being my big break. But I had to be careful, because if it all went pear shaped I could be in for a big fall. For the next stage I had to travel to Birmingham City football ground and it would be a matter of sudden death.

We had now been whittled down to about 200 people all vying for the five different parts. The producers of Emmerdale wanted a new family that consisted of Mum, Dad, two daughters and one son. I was in the 'Father' category even though I was clearly ten years younger than any of the other wanabe fathers. This didn't faze me though and at the next audition I started to really enjoy the process. I began flirting with the female judge after noticing that she had taken a shine to me.

I was determined to just be myself and didn't try to be some kind of 'Luvvie' like a lot of the others were which was getting them noticed for all the wrong reasons.

I didn't have any problem with my acting ability and at the end of the day when we were separated into two groups; I hoped and prayed that this was going to be my big break. One group was to stay and the other, to go home. We were kept waiting for what seemed ages and just as the stress reached its climax we were brought together for their decision. "Ok you guys," said Nasty Nikki, a name the papers had given the female judge following on from Nasty Nigel in Popstars. "You lot on the left," she said (that was my group) "Well first let me say well done for getting this far…"

"Oh s**t," I thought "I'm on my way home."

"…and whatever happens, don't worry because you're coming back again!" she said with a big grin on her face and looking directly at me. I couldn't believe it. It was another yes! Everyone screamed for joy, whilst the losers looked on defeated. I had done it again. "Could this really be my year?" I asked myself, not sure whether to believe it or not. I didn't want to put all my hopes into one basket so to speak but it was difficult not to. If I did and it didn't work out how low would I go? Before when

I had said "Maybe this time I'm gonna make it", I hadn't really meant it. But now it looked more real than ever, I could almost touch it.

There were two more sets of auditions before the final choice was made and throughout the whole process we were all being filmed for the TV program 'Soapstars' that would go out on ITV later that year. It was pretty much a forerunner to 'X Factor' in its format. I had been filmed quite a lot and knew that the makers of the program liked me as I was the only 'Geezer' on the show and made good TV. I tried to play this to my advantage. Who knows, if I didn't go all the way and got good airtime anyway I could still get an agent and get work from it as a result.

The first set of final auditions was held in London and we were all given rooms at a five star hotel on the Thames. We would be working with other people again and this time we had to do a screen kiss.

I was teamed up with a middle aged bank cashier from up north who was so nervous beforehand that she drank half a bottle of wine. I had given her lessons in what to do, (and I don't mean practicing). I had told her how best to do a screen kiss so we didn't look like we were doing it for the first time.

Then we were on. Lights, camera, action. The whole shebang. The script went well and both of us remembered our lines, then it came to the kiss. It was ok but I didn't like doing it, as it was so clinical. Anyway we left to applause and had a break before another five hours of gruelling auditions.

I was having a blast while I was there and became known very quickly for being the life and soul of the party; of course fuelled by copious amounts of alcohol. I was hung over every day and to be honest I don't know how I got through it. I was so mentally and emotionally drained from my lifestyle and being in an atmosphere of suspense which the judges created was awful, plus not knowing if you were going to be rejected by them on national TV. All that as well as dealing with the negativity racing around in my own head was torture.

Finally decision time had arrived and after much sweating and mental torture I was through again. I was stunned into silence. I didn't think I was going to get through the first audition never mind make it this far but inside me expectation was building as my hopes and dreams were getting nearer by the hour.

I went home to many accolades and was due to go to Leeds for the final stretch in two weeks so had plenty of time to get myself prepared. I was so convinced I was going to hit the big time that I started telling everyone I had got the part and began living like a star. The two weeks flew by and before I knew it I was in Leeds feeling optimistic about my future. We all met at a hotel and spent the night in the bar talking about our chances and there was a real buzz about the place as everyone wanted it so badly.

The producers had a fun packed schedule for us the next day and we went off to the Emmerdale village to be shown around where we could possibly be filming if we got the part.

Later that day they held some of the auditions at the holiday village, which was sometimes used in the program. When I had finished mine I went into a holding room where everyone was sat waiting their turn to see the judges and get the "yes you're staying" or "sorry you're going home". When I had been in and got the all clear I was so full of excitement I ran down the corridor bursting through the double doors to the waiting room and shouted, "Who's the daddy! Who's the daddy!" much to everyone's amusement. I felt unstoppable and things just kept slotting into place. I'd now got through so many rounds that there were only three or four potential dads left and to be honest, I thought I was better than all of them!

It didn't last long though and I was only there for one more day before I started feeling I was on my way home. People were trying to reassure me saying, "Don't worry, they won't kick you out you're going all the way." I wasn't so sure though and lo and behold I didn't get through the next round. Right at the final stages I was called into the judge's room and told by Nikki, "Sorry you've not been chosen. Anyway you'd be better off in Eastenders." Just my f**king luck. I went back in the waiting room and told the others that it was all over for me. So close yet so far. Everyone was shocked that I was going and all the positive emotions that had built up in me evaporated in a millisecond. I left p***ed off but not surprised that my dream had evaded me once again. But even though I didn't get in at Emmerdale my journey was far from over!

The program aired on ITV a few months later and the attention it brought me was phenomenal. Over ten million people watched the show each week in the UK and as a result I was getting noticed in the streets. People were shouting, "Who's the daddy!" One time I even got mobbed in Leicester's Shires shopping centre by a load of mums and their kids wanting autographs.

It was hectic but I loved it and wanted more. I thought I had been cut out to be famous or to be a nobody. I could never be anywhere in between. But even though I had got some of the attention I desired and my life had changed a little on the outside, my life after Soapstars continued the same way as before. It was now easier than ever to get freebies after being on TV and I soon took full advantage of the situation. Lots of drinking, even more cocaine and gambling like a mad man.

By this time I had received an invitation to meet an agent in London as a direct result of having been seen on Soapstars.

I went to see him and after a lengthy meeting he agreed to take me on. He sent me to see loads of different people he knew in the business, people at the BBC, ITV and also some casting agents for adverts.

One of the casting agents Paul DeFratas was on the panel in the Soapstars program and after a 'casting' (audition) to play a father in a Matalan advert he called me to say I'd got the part. I was in Argos at the time and let out a loud "Fantastic!" in the middle of the shop. I'm sure the other shoppers thought "I'll have whatever he's got if it's that good." I was going to get 1800 quid for the day and I wasn't about to turn that down.

It meant another trip down to London which was becoming a regular thing now and I even considered moving back down there but never had enough money. I went down the following week to do the shoot and it went well. I was treated like a star and I loved it. The advert was shown on TV quite soon afterwards thus adding to my newfound fame, but still, it didn't end there.

After auditions for the Bill on ITV and Doctors on BBC1, I landed another two roles, they weren't massive but I was in three episodes of the Bill and one for Doctors, both being full on acting parts with dialogue.

I remember on one of the shoots we were filming in a rough council estate in Wimbledon. The whole neighbourhood came out to watch us filming and after we'd finished a long queue of people formed waiting to get their pictures taken with me and to get autographs, it was crazy. I loved being on set and I felt at home in front of the camera and even though people were recognising me, I still hadn't done anything big enough to be recognised within the industry to secure a long term contract and make me rich enough to stop worrying. People on the street and back home were treating me differently though. Suddenly I had loads of 'friends' and getting drugs and booze was a doddle.

By this time my relationship with Kate was at breaking point. All the money I'd earnt from TV went straight to her to repay what I had borrowed and I was always left with nothing. I had to keep borrowing more on the promise that I was going to land a big enough role to put things straight.

The next few months work was a bit bare and I spent most of my time capitalising on my 'local celebrity' status, trying to get by as best I could.

I was still on a real high after my new found stardom. Surely nothing can go wrong now. I was having the time of my life. Not only did they not go wrong, they began to get even better. I received another call from my agent asking me to go to London to read for a part in a new TV series called Paradise Heights on BBC1.

I went down there knowing I had to make a good impression. I met the casting agents in their office on Charlotte St in London. They were a family run business and I was introduced to the agent doing the casting. Dan Hubbard of Hubbard Casting. We got on really well and after the casting I stayed around to chat for a while. He showed me what he had just finished working on and pulled out some pictures of a load of blokes in weird clothes. He said the film was called 'Lord of the Rings' and they had been filming in New Zealand. I didn't think anything of it at the time and continued our conversation (I wish I'd asked for some of the original shots now).

I went home and a few days later my agent called. "Johnny," he said, "Dan thought you were a really nice guy and wants to use you in the program, although you didn't get the part you went for, but he has another smaller part for you to play, what you think?"

I was just happy to be working as I had run out of cash again and needed a job badly so I said "That's great, when do I start and how much do I get paid?" It turned out I was going to get about two grand for eleven days shooting which was to start almost immediately.

They had a caravan for me to use on the film set and I was going to be playing a security guard who worked for a gangster alongside Neil Morrissey, Charles Dale and Ralph Little. It was bizarre on set. There I was rehearsing with guys I had seen on TV so many times before. I never thought I would ever meet them never mind be acting with them, it was crazy but great.

Anyway, I tried to fit in as best I could and to be fair they were all really nice guys which made it much easier. After the second day of filming, Charles Dale, a tall guy with short mousy hair and a goatee beard who used to be in Coronation Street, asked me "Where are you staying down here?" I told him that I was sleeping in the caravan on set, as I couldn't afford a hotel in the West End at the prices they were charging. He seemed genuinely concerned as it was freezing cold at the time and the caravan I was staying in wasn't the warmest of places. And later that day, as things were drawing to an end he asked me if I would like to stay at his apartment in the City as his agent had negotiated it in with his fee and it would get me out of the cold for at least one night.

"That would be great," I said. I thought it might also be an opportunity to get him to put in a good in word for me with future producers and writers.

We got in his limo and headed off towards Lambeth Bridge stopping along the way at an off licence for some beers. When we got there he took me up to the fifth floor and showed me into his apartment. It was stunning, a really posh gaff. As we walked in he just said the word 'Lights' and the lights came on. It was so cool. We had a beer and looked out across the Thames which was lit up with the coloured lights from the clubs and bars shimmering on the water. What made it more amazing was the fact that the walls throughout the whole apartment were made of glass giving us spectacular views of the whole city, it was a seriously trendy gaff and seemed a million miles away from the reality of the streets below that I knew so well.

As I looked out across the city, I could see the area where I'd once slept rough and couldn't quite take in how things had changed. I said to Charles as I pointed, "See over there by those buildings, I used to sleep rough there and if you had told me a year ago that I'd be up here drinking beer with you and playing a part in a TV program, I would have said you were crazy." Charles shook his head in amazement at my story, or at least the story I had up until then.

I slept well that night in a great big bed under what felt like very expensive sheets and bed covers and awoke to the smell of success and some bacon of course. I could get used to this I thought as we got into the car and headed for the set. It was early morning and after staying with Charles I felt more accepted by the other actors, as if I was one of the gang. After a quick cup of tea, the producer wanted to crack on with it so things hurried along from that point.

The rest of the shoot went well and without a hitch, and of course not wanting to miss an opportunity, I managed to get both Neil and Ralph's phone number. We all said our goodbyes and parted company. I went back to Leicester with my head held high and hoped that this wouldn't be the end of my budding career. I knew I was going to see them again as we had arranged to meet up at the cast party some months later and by the time it came round I had been paid for the job and blown the money several times over gambling, no surprise there then! That month I took Kate to the party and we got totally trashed on gear (coke). I was trying to forget all the crap I'd been through and was desperately trying to cling on to the little success I had. Coke and booze weren't the answer but at least they helped me forget for a while.

It was a mad night; we were all hammered and were messing around on the dance floor trying to break dance. We ended up going back to a hotel with some well-known celebrities to smoke some weed. "I don't fancy any of the crap" I said, convinced I was better than that, yet I was going crazy trying to get some more charley but to no avail, so we just went back to our own hotel completely knackered and I necked a load of sleeping tablets to try and slow my heart down enough to sleep.

I carried on following the same pattern as always when I got home. Getting by on money I begged, stole or borrowed. This was when my gambling became totally out of control and I even started dealing drugs to pay for my lavish lifestyle. I was taking about two and a half grams of coke per day for about two thirds of the week and the rest of the time was spent recovering from the effects of coming down off the gear and being malnourished as I wouldn't eat for days.

At the time I was getting serious liver pains and would pass blood in my urine. This was caused by the ridiculous amounts of alcohol I could consume when out of it on coke. You see the problem was, that I would go out and drink until I could drink no more and was usually p***ed out of my head by about eight o'clock. So to enable me to see the night through I would do line after line of coke, which would almost instantly sober me up and give me the ability to drink doubles and trebles without even being affected. Taking coke was so addictive. I would salivate at the mere thought of having a line and if I knew someone had some in the pub or bar I was in, I would pester them and pester them until they gave me some. When that white powder hit the back of your nose and slid down your throat, instantly numbing it, it delivered the best rush you could ever experience. It was 100% pure unadulterated ecstasy. But one line was never enough for me and I had fallen under its spell. I would take so much that my whole body would literally be shaking and I would have to stuff bog roll up my nose to stem the flow of the constant nosebleeds. This would go on all night and by the time I'd get home it would be around seven the next morning because I'd always end up at some other coke head's house drinking Jack Daniels and talking b****x till the early hours. I would walk back home in broad daylight, passing normal people on their way to work. My body was totally f***ed. My kidneys would be aching and my p**s would be so dark it looked like treacle. I was in a terrible state and became so paranoid about dying that I'd go to sleep with my hand on my chest so I could feel my heart beating. On top of all that, I was getting involved with the wrong kind of people now and my status from local celebrity quickly dissolved and I became the local joke. No body wanted to know me anymore and I was fast becoming mentally unstable.

17

Trying to subdue me

If only I could get help and support, things might change I thought in a positive way only for it to be quickly replaced by a torrent of negativity. I could never seem to hold onto positive words long enough to make a difference. I was at an all time low. Kate was away in Hong Kong on business and I was left to my own devices, which was never a good idea. I was making a small amount of money from cutting the coke I was buying with creatine powder, as the crystals in creatine looked just like Charlie and if I got the mix right you couldn't really tell how s**t it was.

That weekend I went out as usual and ran into a guy that I knew who also was on the gear. His name was Steve; he was tall and muscular and looked a bit like Nicholas Cage. Like me when he was sober he was a nice guy but he was having problems at home and his business wasn't doing too well. This wasn't good, both of us fuelled by coke and unhappiness decided to go on a three day bender consuming about six grams of Charlie each and about five bottles of gin between us without eating any food. Those few days were a blur and kind of blended into one, everything seemed like a horrible déjà vu.

When I finally went home I was completely off my face and my mind was fragmented like a broken pane of glass.

It was about three in the morning and my head just wouldn't slow down, not surprising really after all the gear I'd done and even though I was feeling so bad my chaotic thoughts wouldn't relent, constantly barraging my mind, telling me "You're going to die, you just felt a pain in your chest, you're going to have a heart attack!"

I didn't know what to do, I just wanted to escape this misery but my heart kept on beating faster and faster, pumping this devil's dandruff (coke) through my veins and round my exhausted body. In a desperate attempt to get help I called the Samaritans. I tried to explain how I felt but by this time I could hardly string a sentence together. It was no use so I put the phone down. Then I felt another sharp pain in my chest "You're having a heart attack," I thought, believing the lies in my head. "No! I can't die, not yet." I grabbed the phone and called an ambulance.

"Help me, I've had too much coke, I'm going to die!" I said to the operator only just managing to get the words out.

Things became very hazy from then on and I don't remember much after that. I was picked up by an ambulance and taken to hospital. Throughout the whole ordeal I was not compos mentis. Only when getting back home and seeing the neighbours standing outside their homes looking on with concern did I realise the seriousness of what had happened.

"Are you alright?" asked an old bloke from across the street. I nodded but said nothing and went inside.

"I don't want to talk about it," I grunted at the ambulance man who had brought me back. When they left I went to bed and finally got some rest.

During this whole period I was taking an anti-depressant drug called Seroxat. I later found out through watching a Panorama documentary that whilst taking these drugs many people had committed suicide and some had even snapped, killing their partners or family for no apparent reason. This was a shocking revelation and makes me even more amazed that I'm alive today to write this book.

By the following weekend I had recovered enough to have a few drinks, convincing myself that I wouldn't go as far as last time.

Kate was still away and was due back the following Monday. While she was gone she had left me her silver VW Polo to use. I had been out in town that day and had seen a mate, Lee who was at a loose end. Lee was a slimy looking guy with black slicked back hair and glasses and although he was a very likeable character, he was a notoriously heavy drinker round town.

I invited him round our house for a drink, as it was a glorious sunny day. He agreed and on the way back we stopped off and bought some vodka. We sat in the garden drinking and having a right laugh but soon we had got through the booze and wanted more. Lee suggested we go to town and he'd buy me a couple of beers. I thought it was a great idea, of course and said I'd drive. I felt fine and not drunk at all. We jumped into the car and sped off down the road laughing and joking. I was doing about 50 mph in a 30 mph zone and as I took the corner I clipped the curb hit a bollard and flipped the car upside down landing on top of a parked vehicle. Both cars were a right mess. I was stuck and as I opened my eyes I saw a number of vehicles screeching to a halt. 'Oh shit I've really gone and f***ed things up now', and before I could move and make my escape the fire service were at the scene. I closed my eyes and pretended to be unconscious then heard a guy shout, "It's my cousin" as he ran over to me. It was my cousin Mark who was a fireman from the local station at South Wigston just down the road from the crash and it just so happened that he was on duty that day. I felt so embarrassed and kept still avoiding any conversation.

They had to cut me from the wreckage and I was taken to hospital with a police escort, as they wanted to check if I had been drinking when I 'came round'. We got to the hospital and I was checked over and left on a trolley as the police chatted with the doctors.

I lay there; still, gently opening my eyes just enough to peek through my eye lashes so that I could see who was where. I could see the police were about forty feet away at the end of the corridor. I knew my way around the hospital and because I was still p***ed, thought I could do a runner. I waited till I thought they weren't looking and jumped up off the trolley legging it as fast as I could down the corridor. The police sprang into action and were on top of me within seconds. One of the coppers rugby tackled me to the ground and I kicked and screamed, swearing at the top of my voice and trying to get him off. They didn't mess around though and two or three of them grabbed my arms trying to subdue me. They banged the cuffs on and closed them really tight cutting off the blood to my hands. It was really painful and they knew it, lifting me up by the cuffs causing me to cry out in pain.

"Loosen the f***ing cuffs you t**ts!" I shouted at the top of my voice. "Come on" I screamed. "Right I'm not going anywhere 'til you loosen the cuffs", and with that I relaxed all my body muscles causing my legs to drag on the floor trying to be as heavy as possible for them. They were all big lads and it didn't seem to stop them dragging me towards the pig van waiting outside. One of them said, "Pick your legs up," in an aggressive tone as he yanked me about. "Loosen the cuffs then" I yelped in pain. They ignored me and threw me into the back of the van with the cuffs still really tight and slammed the door. I began kicking the metal cage inside, overtaken by anger.

"Get these f***ing cuffs of me you b***ards" I demanded.

I continued shouting abuse at the police all the way to the cop shop and told them what I was going to do to them when I was released. They didn't take kindly to the threats and showed me no mercy when they got me out and into reception. After checking me in, they gave me no other option but to do a breath test so I took it hoping for the best.

Bad news. I was way over the limit and was now in big trouble. They obviously took what I said seriously about fighting them if they took my cuffs off so took no chances with me and after giving me a quick check over and removing my trainers they slung me in a cell holding me down on the floor whilst they removed the restraints.

"Let me out you w***ers!" I shouted banging my head against the cell door; they didn't respond and left me alone to sober up and calm down from my drunken temper.

I spent the whole night in there making noise and shouting until the early hours when sleep finally got the better of me. In the morning I was woken by the sound of the metal shutter in the door being opened and a cup of tea being pushed through. I looked up and saw a piece of paper that had been left next to the plastic cup. I got up and had a look. It looked like a birthday card and had a picture of a cross on the front and read 'Jesus loves you...'

I opened it and looked inside and to my surprise it read, '...but we all think you're a t**t!'

I smiled wryly, "Very funny." I shouted, directing my sarcasm in their general direction. I heard the coppers laughing in the background amused by their prank. Little did they know that one day my life would be changed beyond recognition by those very words, 'Jesus loves you!'

Eventually I was charged with drink driving and let out on bail. I felt like s**t and had a stinking hangover as I usually did after a night in the cells. I made my way home thinking how on earth am I going to explain this to Kate when she gets back. I thought it best to call her before she left Hong Kong hoping she'd have time to calm down before she got back. It went down like a sack of s**t and she wasn't happy at all. I realised this was probably the final nail in the coffin as far as our relationship was concerned and waited at home anxiously hoping that things would work out.

When she got back we had an almighty row almost immediately and during our argument things were said from both parties about our unhappiness in the relationship. She wanted me out and I didn't have a leg to stand on, she owned the house and all the contents. I had jack s**t to my name and in fact was in debt to her.

"I can't take any more", she said, crying her eyes out.

"So what are you going do?" I asked. "Kick me out on the streets?"

"There's no other way" she sobbed.

"Fine", I said in defiance and stormed out. Some hours later after I had calmed down I returned to the house. Kate wasn't in and there on the table was a roll mat used for sleeping outdoors, a sleeping bag and seventy quid. I knew what this meant; I had been there many times before. It was time to go. Once again I was homeless but where was I going to go this time?

My heart sank and I let out a long sigh. F***ing hell not again. The only place I thought I could go where I could maybe get myself out the s**t was London. I'd got into a hostel down there before and was re-housed as a result of it so if I could do it again, I know I could get things right. I had been in this position so many times before and knew that somehow I could turn things round but one thing was for sure, whatever happens it certainly wouldn't be boring.

An idea came to me. I had always liked the thought of making a documentary out of my life as so many crazy things had happened to me and what better time than now? I had been watching Richard and Judy some days earlier and they were always sending people out with a camcorder to film wacky things in their lives so I gave them a call. I talked to a woman at Channel Four and explained that I had been in the Bill and Soapstars etc and told her my predicament but to my surprise they weren't interested.

"Your loss" I said cockily as I put the phone down. The fact that they weren't interested just added fuel to the fire. Being rejected for me was a fact of life. F**k them then. I'll show them! Right, I thought. It was time to go.

I grabbed the few little things I had and left, making my way to the train station. The train for London pulled up and I climbed on board. 'Goodbye Leicester' I said leaning out of the window as the train pulled off. I vowed that when I come back I *will* be a success and that I'd never return amidst the same sorry circumstances.

There was no ticket inspector in sight so after buying a couple of beers I found a seat and relaxed knowing I had a free ride. Thank God for small mercies.

I looked out of the window and watched the world rush by. I could see people walking their dogs, houses with lights on and people inside getting on with their lives. Everyone seemed so settled and content. What on earth had happened to me? As my eyes focused I saw my own reflection in the glass and was shocked at how rough I looked and began thinking about my life and what the future might hold. Would I ever be content? Or was I destined to die an early, unfulfilled death? Only time would tell. I still had so much life to give.

18

Prêt a manger

It was dark when the train pulled into St. Pancras Station and I was in no rush so I let the other passengers get off first. I strolled down the platform hoping for some divine intervention. Maybe a thought or an idea would just come to me and everything would work out. Nothing came.

I made my way to the area I knew best, the West End. The bright lights and glamour of the Capital were so hypnotic and for the first couple of hours I hit the bars. If it wasn't for the fact I was carrying a sleeping bag and roll mat I would have forgotten that I was homeless. People just seem happier down here I thought, as I drank my beer and looked round the room and I want some of it.

I spent the first few nights sleeping rough and was drinking with the little money I had left. After one particularly heavy night I started feeling really rough and thought I'd better go and see if there were any hostels that were taking in.

I started off by going back to St. Mungos but they were full so I headed up to Soho and found a hostel on Dean St. right near the corner of Oxford St. They were taking in and had a room available the next day and, as I had been the first to enquire I would get first refusal if I returned the following morning. I headed off into town still feeling a little dejected but hoped that tomorrow would bring me better luck.

By now I'd had nothing to eat for a couple of days and, with no money, was desperate to get something inside me. I roamed around the shops looking for opportunities to steal something either to eat or to sell and ended up outside a Prêt a Manger (Sandwich shop) in Leicester Square. The staff were very busy and people were coming in and going out pretty much un-noticed. "This is the one," I thought trying to find the balls to go and do it. I had nothing to lose, what did I care anyway? I had nowhere to live and if I got arrested at least I'd have a nice warm cell. I went in and bottled it coming straight out again. "Come on you've got to do this," I told myself, knowing that if I kept walking in and out I'd draw attention to myself.

I went in again but this time I went straight up to the section where the sandwiches and cans of drink were. There were loads of people grabbing stuff from the shelves and taking them over to the tills and lots more people eating their food at tables near by.

"They wouldn't do anything if they saw you pinching surely? People in London wouldn't react if you dropped dead in front of them." I thought trying to reassure myself. "Just do it," came a voice from inside. I grabbed a chicken and avocado sandwich and a can of pop and my heart was beating like I'd just run a hundred meters. And as casually as I could I walked out of the shop and round the corner into the crowds of tourists. I had done it and hadn't been caught. The buzz was amazing like a drug rushing through my veins. I could certainly do that again. What a rush! As soon as I was out of sight of the shop I stuffed the food into my mouth taking huge bites smiling from ear to ear pleased with the results of my sticky fingers. The sandwich was gorgeous and went down a treat and as I sat there for a while watching the world go by, for a few short minutes I didn't need anything and forgot about the fact that I had no money, nowhere to stay and, at that precise moment in time, no idea who I was or what the future held.

19
Charity

That night I slept outside the hostel, I felt completely f***ed in my head and was becoming more and more unstable by the second. Not knowing who I was and having no future had been playing with my mind all night. By morning, negativity and depression were spreading through my brain like a cancer, eating up any remnants of positive thought I had left (if I had any at all). As soon as the day staff arrived I was let in and given a single room on the fifth floor. The hostel was all-male and had approximately ninety residents. I'd been warned by the staff to keep a low profile and watch my back, as the day before, one of the residents had been murdered in the communal TV lounge for changing the TV channel without asking. It doesn't take much to send some people over the edge does it! The murderer had been watching his favourite program and apparently after someone got up and changed the channel, the killer protested, and then left the room only to return moments later with a huge carving knife. He then set about his victim and fatally stabbed him in the chest. This was serious stuff and when I was shown to my room I felt a shiver go down my spine, imagining what had taken place only hours before.

My room was pretty much like any other hostel room I'd been in before. It had a single metal-framed bed, wardrobe, sink, and a small window that over looked a jazz bar on Dean Street.

I took on board what they said and for the first few weeks kept myself quiet, trying to suss out the other residents.

I got on with the hostel staff quite well, some of them had even seen me on TV, which was weird, and when they mentioned it I felt a mixture of shame, pride and embarrassment.

"I'm not down I'm either up or getting up," I told them, desperately looking for a way to justify my being there. One particular lady was so enamoured with meeting me that she asked for my autograph and took my photo,

"It may be worth something one day," she said putting it up behind the counter in reception.

"Yeah right," I said laughing nervously, knowing that I had reached great heights and had achieved something, yet here I was at the very bottom again.

There were some pretty mean looking guys in there and as I was quite stocky, I got some attention from one or two that were trying to assert their authority, but I didn't really care about all that crap and spent most of my days out of the hostel trying to get money to feed my habits.

One day, in a desperate attempt to get some cash to fund my addictions, me and a couple of other lads Al and Bob decided to nick some charity boxes from a well known charity shop in Leicester Square, rather than doing something else a little more risky. There was about two quid in copper coins in mine and the other guys had about seven quid between them, hardly the great train robbery was it? Anyway, we soon spent that and whilst drinking our loot away Al had an idea that, if successful, could prove to be a bit more lucrative. It would cost us an initial outlay but the return would be much greater. He said that if we got some t-shirts printed with 'Help The Homeless' on them and used the library internet to find a template for ID tags, we could print labels that would go over the charity box labels we stole, and could go out collecting round the streets and in the bars, even do all the shops in the West End and make a packet.

Technically we wouldn't be lying, as you couldn't get any more homeless than we were.

"So what do you think?" He said. There was a short silence as we thought it over then we all agreed emphatically that we were up for it.

A few days later when Al got his Giro he used some of the cash to pay for all the bits we needed. The t-shirts looked great and we wore them with a sense of pride. It was as if we were doing the community a favour by asking for cash to support ourselves rather than going out robbing shops and mugging people. I suppose we were. There was no question of moral standards as we could very easily justify what we were doing and not one of us felt guilty at the time. In fact quite the opposite, and when we went on the streets we became so good at what we were doing it was almost professional. It was easy acting like we worked for a real charity and whilst asking for donations our personalities changed and we became very official and polite, we would do anything to extract money from people. You would never have known we were homeless ourselves.

"Oh, the homeless have such a hard time of it, someone's got to look after them." I would say to a shop keeper as he was stuffing ten quid in my tin. "Thank you, and God bless you," I would call as I was leaving the shop helping myself to a couple of chocolate bars on the way out.

One time I was in Soho Square and noticed a limo pulling up outside the Twentieth Century Fox building in an area well known for directors and high profile actors. I ran over to the car and who should pop out but Ben Kingsley, the Oscar winning actor who played Ghandi.

"Hi Mr Kingsley," I said, getting his attention by rattling my tin.

"Hello," he replied and immediately I went into my life story telling him all about being kicked out of RADA and how I'd been on TV and about my drug and drink problems. I don't think he really knew what to say although he was very polite and was quite impressed by the fact I'd been to RADA.

I asked him if he knew anyone who might give me my big break and he replied "You know, you would be good in a Ken Loach film. Give me your number and if I get time I will see what I can do." I couldn't believe it and wrote out my number handing it to him sharpish.

"Thanks ever so much," I shouted as he disappeared into the building. F***ing hell! Ben Kingsley! That was pretty amazing and he put a fiver in my tin as well. What a result.

I went off and told the others that I'd got five quid out of Ghandi and they couldn't believe it either. We went to a bench and sat down counting our takings. I'd got forty-five quid and felt my luck was in so it was off to the bookies 'to win some money'. Even after such a strange and fortuitous day I still managed to turn my good fortune into bad and came out of the bookies with only enough change for a couple of cheap cans. Yet again after all my hard work I was getting poorer and Ladbrokes were getting richer. Even though the charity work was going quite well, we very quickly ran out of places to go and eventually it fizzled out.

Over the next couple of months I managed to fund myself on crisis loans from the social and when that dried up I sold my passport to one of the bigger guys in the hostel. Jimmy was a big black guy, he had told me he would get me fifty quid for it from some guy he knew in China Town. A week had gone by since he had made that promise and I hadn't seen him or the cash so naturally was getting a little p***ed off. When I saw him in the canteen at tea time the next day I went over to where he was sat and he turned round and looked me up and down like I was a piece of s**t. I didn't know what to do so I said "Come and see me later I want to talk to you." There were about five other residents at his table and a canteen full of guys. Wanting to scare me and look big in front of the other blokes he stood up and got right in my face. He was much taller than me about six foot four and pretty intimidating. He pointed to himself and said aggressively, "You want some of this. Do you?" Then he started laughing, thinking I was going to just disappear. To be honest I wanted to disappear, I wanted the floor to open up and swallow me. Feeling afraid but not wanting to show it I turned my back on him and sat down. Inside I was fuming and knew that if I showed any sign of weakness he would walk all over me and I could kiss my passport money goodbye.

I began eating my food and listened to the laughter coming from his table. I was going over various scenarios in my head where I was bigger than he was or maybe where I was a karate expert and kicked his head in while he was begging me for mercy. Then I came back to reality and found myself angrier than ever. I finished my grub then washed my knife, fork and spoon and went to my room.

I knew I had to do something about that t**t. The thoughts in my head were telling me to go down and confront him. I'd got myself into such a frenzy I grabbed the knife I had just used for dinner and started back down the stairs; my mind was in turmoil. One thought would be of 'What are you doing? This could go horribly wrong' whilst another would tell me to 'Just do it'. Which thought do I listen to?

I slowed down as I got to the canteen and peered through the reinforced window in the door. There he was, as bold as brass sat in the same spot talking the same old crap. Before I could stop myself I opened the door enough for my head to get through and called him.

"Jimmy come here, now", I shouted, staring at him with a hard glare. He looked shocked by my tone but didn't move. I closed the door and put the knife in my back pocket. Did he think I was soft? I opened the door again and shouted "Jimmy, f***ing get over here now!" This time I'd got his attention. He got up and started walking over. I let the door close and shut my eyes, getting myself ready to rumble; when I opened them there he was standing right in front of me. I wasted no time and screamed at him,

"Where's my f***ing passport you s**t head? I'm not messing about anymore." He saw my hand move behind me to my back pocket and I thought this is it, it's do or die. But his reaction took me by surprise.

"Please don't hurt me," he begged. He was almost child like. I wasn't sure if it was for real or not at first.

"I will get your passport back or give you the money, I don't want any trouble" he continued pleading and gesturing with his hands.

To be honest I was completely thrown by this and wasn't sure what to do. I hadn't expected that at all. All I could say was, "Well you'd better or else there's gonna be trouble." I gave him a mean stare and walked off.

My heart was beating like a drum and back in my room I felt mixed feelings about what had just taken place. I was full of adrenaline and on a 'Victory high', yet I felt kind of sad at the same time. I'd messed up big time getting myself in such a situation and letting myself fall so low again. "This s**t can't happen again," I told myself. I couldn't believe how far I was willing to go!

There must be a way to get out of here. After calming down I sat on the bed and picked up the 'Stage' newspaper I'd bought hoping I would spot something worthwhile in there. When suddenly it hit me.

20

Fifteen to one

There staring me in the face was an advert for singers/actors to go and work on a cruise ship. "Now, that's what I'm talking about!" Getting excited about the prospect of leaving this s**t hole and sailing the high seas. Surely it couldn't be any worse than it was here. Jobs in the Stage get filled very quickly as there are so many wanabe and unemployed entertainers in London, so I called that evening and spoke to some Scottish chap (called Steve) who asked if I'd like to go down to see him for an audition/interview the next day. He seemed nice and I was really excited although somewhat nervous about singing, as I hadn't sung in front of anyone for some time, well at least not sober anyway.

"Right, ok what am I gonna wear?" I asked myself. I didn't have any nice clothes as I'd left them all in Leicester so I did the best with what I'd got and the next day made my way down there. I arrived at the building where he had told me to go and was told to wait in the reception area.

"Hi Johnny" a guy said, I knew it was him by his accent and shook his hand "Well done for finding us" he said. "Would you like to come through and have a wee chat?" He led the way up some stairs and into a large office. I looked around and saw pictures on the walls of various cruise ships and teams of entertainers that had worked on them. Right in front of me was a large model of a ship on his desk. This looks good, I thought, this could be my ticket out of here. We had a long chat and talked about all the acting work I'd done before and he seemed suitably impressed with it. I had been there about five minutes when his phone rang. He asked if it was ok to take it and chatted on the phone for a while. When he had finished he said, "Sorry about that Johnny, that was my boss and I've got to go and sort some things out so we'll have to leave it there for now and we'll get in touch" With that he showed me out.

I walked off down the road feeling dejected. It seemed that it was over before it had begun and I didn't even get to sing. I caught the bus back to the hostel and went to my room. It was a sunny day; I opened the window and slumped on my bed. I was just nodding off when my mobile rang. I looked at the screen; it said 'withheld number'. Normally I wouldn't answer those kind of calls because nine times out of ten it was a debt collecting agency or someone I didn't want to talk to but for some reason I pressed answer.

"Hello," I said, half expecting to hear, "Jonathan Kinch we have been trying to get hold of you for blah, blah, blah." But to my surprise it was Steve, the guy from the Cruise Company. He said that he had great news for me. He said that he actually thought that I was over qualified for the position of entertainer and therefore thought I'd be better suited as an assistant cruise director and asked if I'd like to go and work on board the Pride of Bilbao for P&O co-ordinating all the acts on their three day mini cruises from Portsmouth to Northern Spain. "Would I!" I thought, trying to contain the rush of energy that had just coursed through my body. "That would be great," I replied, trying to sound professional.

"I see here that you live in Soho, mmm, very posh. Ok we'll send details in the post of where and when."

"Great," I replied "See you soon." He put the phone down and I paused for a moment letting what had just happened sink in, then let out an almighty "Yes!" I was getting out of here, I couldn't believe it. He thought I lived in a posh area, if he only knew the truth. Well who cares now? I was on cloud nine and for the next few days waiting for the letter to arrive life was good.

When the letter came I opened it excitedly. Wow, the ship looked fantastic. It was massive. I was to get my own cabin, a uniform and thirteen hundred quid a month, I was well chuffed. As I read on my heart sunk. There was a big problem. They needed me to have at least two smart suits as I would be greeting the passengers and hosting the main events in the evening and I had to have a passport! That dickhead Jimmy hadn't returned mine or given me the money. S**t! I thought. What could I do now? My mind was racing trying to think of how I could sort this out. I had two weeks to come up with a solution or everything was down the pan.

Then completely out of the blue I remembered when I was in the library some years ago looking for funding for RADA an article I had seen about the Actors Benevolent Fund. The ABF was a group of people who helped actors and performers who were out-of-work or in difficult circumstances to get back on their feet. If I could get in touch with them and show them this letter of acceptance with a covering letter from the hostel they might be able to help me.

I went to see the staff and told them my situation; it was easy getting a covering letter from them, as they were as keen for me to move on as I was. I asked if I could call the ABF from the staff phone, as this would support my story of being homeless and how I was actively looking to get back to work. Reluctantly they agreed.

My call was answered by a receptionist who listened to my story and said she thought they could help. She arranged an interview with me for the following day and asked me to bring all the relevant information to support my claims.

The next day I got up early and, having no bus fare, made my way down there on foot. "Right, come on Kinchie," I said. "Don't cock this up. This is another golden opportunity." Keen to get in there and seal the deal, I arrived a little early.

"Hi, it's Mr Kinch," I said as I pressed the buzzer for their office, "I have an appointment for 9.30."

"Ok, come on up. Second floor," came a voice from the intercom, as the door was buzzed open. I went to the reception.

"Mr Finch?" asked the lady behind the desk

"Er, it's Kinch actually and yes it's me," I said trying to sound jolly and not offended.

"Take a seat," she said. I sat down and was told the main man would be in shortly and to help myself to water from the cooler if I wanted it. A few minutes later a rather posh, old looking fella, walked in and went straight into the office next to were I was sitting. He looked about sixty-five years old and his half moon glasses were resting on his large hairy nose. He was smartly dressed and had an air of authority about him. The receptionist got up quickly and went in after him, I could hear some mumbling coming from his room and when she returned I was told to go in.

"Sit down Jonathan," he said in a very posh voice "So Jonathan, my name is William. Tell me about yourself and what has brought you here today." That was not a problem for me as I'd told my story many times before and within a few minutes gave him a synopsis of my life to date.

"You've done all that?" he asked in disbelief.

"Yes and more," I said.

"How much do you need," he asked, "The maximum we give is five hundred pounds."

"That should do it," I said showing him my covering letter from the hostel and my letter of acceptance from the cruise company plus a copy of my CV to back up my claims. He sat there for a while perusing my CV and occasionally looking at me over the top of his glasses.

"Well I can see you have definitely done some acting before, and going to RADA, well that is an achievement," he said, "…and living in a hostel you poor thing. Ok, well we have a trustees meeting in a week and we will make a decision then alright?"

"That's great," I said, getting up and shaking his hand. "I look forward to hearing from you."

As I left the room I thought that it had gone quite well.

Bl**dy nice bloke too. If I could get five hundred quid out of him then I could buy some clothes and would have some spendo as well.

The journey back to the hostel went much quicker as my mind was feeding on what could be and for the first time in ages I felt genuinely optimistic about my future. Waiting to hear from them seemed like months but in reality it had only been a week and I had already spent the money ten times over in my head. I had been out looking at mobile phones, suits, new shoes, shirts, the whole shebang.

One afternoon I was called down to reception. Someone was on the phone for me. I picked up the receiver and immediately recognised the posh accent of the trustee from the ABF on the other end of the line. Please let it be good news.

"Hi Jonathan, good news," he said. "We have had our monthly meeting and there has been a unanimous yes to help you out. Obviously we can't give the money to you directly, however, we will be sending one of our trustees shopping with you and he will pay for all your purchases on the ABF credit card is that ok?"

"Yeah that's great," I replied "When can we do it?" We arranged a time for me to meet the guy who was coming out with the credit card and he told me that it was the chap who did the voice over for the TV quiz show 'Fifteen To One'. That was so cool. I used to watch that show every day. I thanked him and said goodbye and I promised to let him know how I got on. At first I was a bit gutted about not being given the cash but it was probably a good idea, as I would have definitely gambled it away.

That week I met Philip, the voice over guy and we went shopping together in the West End. He was such a nice chap and was really help-ful; he even bought me lunch out of his own pocket. I had such a laugh with him and every time he spoke I half expected him to end with "And here's your host Mr William G Stewart!"

It was a great day and I managed to get two great suits, a pair of shoes, three shirts, a tie and a belt. When I walked into the hostel with it all I felt like a normal person again. I was going away. Far away from there and I couldn't wait. It felt like a new adventure was just about to begin and I was leaving the old life behind. Where would this take me though? Only God knew. The next morning I got all dressed up and went and said thank you to all the staff at ABF. They were suitably impressed and wished me good luck on my travels.

A few days later the time had arrived for me to go. I had my bags packed and I was leaving the hostel never to return, in fact, I didn't want to see the inside of a hostel ever again! I put on my suit and went down to reception "You look really smart," said one of the staff members. "Good luck!"

"Thanks," I said, "and thanks for everything. In the nicest possible way, I hope I never see you again." I walked out of the doors with my head held high. "You can't keep a good man down," I thought proudly as I set off on the road to a new life.

21

Nowhere to run

The ship pulled into dock. It was enormous. It must have been like trying to park a block of flats. The ground crew secured it to the dockside with ropes and a gangway was attached to the side. I had to wait till the guy who I was replacing came and got me, so I stood there watching loads of people getting off looking like s**t and pulling trolleys full of fags and booze. These were the types of people who would have been drinking solid for the whole trip. My kind of audience. Then a friendly looking chubby chap walked over to me.

"Johnny?" he asked.

"Yeah, hi," I said.

"Hi, I'm Craig, the guy you'll be replacing," he said "nice to meet you and welcome aboard." He took me onto the ship and we dragged my suitcase through crowds of people who began cheering as Craig went by and thanking him for a great time. The queue to get off seemed never ending, I had no idea there were so many people on board.

I couldn't believe how big this ship was; it was like a maze. How on earth was I going to find my way around here? We eventually got to my cabin which was two decks below the car parking bay and he left me there to unpack. I was literally at the bottom of the ship but I didn't care, I was out of the hostel and starting a new adventure. My cabin was pretty small but it seemed to have everything I needed. There were two bunks that both folded against the wall to make space when needed. There was a small wardrobe and a mirror and a tiny cubicle bathroom, smaller than the hostel but it would do for me.

I took a shower, put my suit on then made my way up to the DJ box in the main theatre. The theatre was huge; it had a large stage with an area where the band could sit and play and seated one thousand people.

Next door was a casino and a load of fruit machines. Just what I needed! I was going to have to steer clear of there.

As we were a vehicle-carrying vessel all crew members, including the entertainment team, were not allowed to drink or use the casino. This was good. It wasn't a matter of trying to avoid gambling or drinking but a direct order. If I got caught I could lose my job and I didn't want that to happen.

The cruise director Marco showed up and introduced me to the team. He was a very smooth, Italian looking bloke with dark swept back hair and olive skin but very nice with it and the rest of the team seemed ok too, well maybe a little bit false but that was to be expected with cruise ship entertainers. We had tea together in the crew canteen and they talked about different shows they had been doing with Craig and how much they were going to miss him. They were clearly very fond of Craig and were wary about anyone taking over his position, which made me feel very uncomfortable, and I began to wish I hadn't come aboard. Every time I'd talk they'd look at me like I had a piece of s**t on my face then start to get really bitchy, and that was just the men! I already wanted to punch someone in the chops and we hadn't even left the dock yet. F***ing hell, I thought. I'm not going to like this and started feeling claustrophobic, wanting to get off.

I went up onto the top deck for some fresh air and saw that we were leaving the bay already and entering the sea. There was no turning back now, reinforcing my feelings of being trapped. Normally in a situation like this I would down tools, so to speak, and do a runner and even though my mind was racing, trying to find a way of getting off the ship it was too late, there was nowhere to run. I had to face my fears and get on with it the best I could. I stayed up there for as long as possible but at 6.30pm the show was due to start and I had to be there to see how things were done.

The ship would set sail from Portsmouth, cross the Bay of Biscay and head over to Northern Spain; it would normally take about three days to get there and back so the trip was advertised as a mini cruise. For the first two runs I would be watching what Craig did and then when he was gone I would be hosting the shows myself. There seemed an awful lot to learn and I desperately wanted to make my mark and show the team that I had what it took to do Craig's job, not just as well as him but better. After the first trip I began to relax and became myself again. I got on with Marco really well and we started to train together in the ship's gym. I had always been keen on weight training but my sporadic lifestyle had put a stop to that.

Now that I wasn't drinking or gambling, at least for the time being, I took it up again and started to get into shape.

At the end of my second run, the job was now officially mine. Craig had gone and I was on my own. I hadn't gambled nor had a drink for a week and as I was so busy focusing on getting my job right I didn't notice it too much. My opening night came and went with great success and I was becoming more confident by the day.

The passengers seemed to warm to me which was good. They were a very mixed group of people, on one hand you would have the stag do's and hen parties, on the other there would be the old people, and from time to time we would take a ship full of leather clad bikers on stunning Harley Davidsons over to Spain. Generally, there wasn't any trouble and by the end of the first two weeks I had made my mark on the job and the team had become more comfortable with my style of working. Every weekend we would swap shifts and the ship would take a different route and go to France on a booze cruise, which was basically a ship full of lager louts who wanted to spend the weekend drinking and pulling girls. This would be the time when one of us would get a chance to get off ship and go into town.

Marco would do the weekend run and I'd go ashore supposedly for some well-deserved rest. At first I did rest but as I became more confident in my job I didn't need to focus so hard and looked elsewhere for my jollies. It wasn't long before I took up my old habits again, drinking stupid amounts of booze, getting off my head on coke and losing all my wages in the bookies every time I'd leave the ship. My gambling and drinking had started to dictate how I lived yet again and as my spending increased I began borrowing money from the other team members and getting increasingly large advances on my wages. This was easy as no one knew about my habits and I was best mates with Marco who had the keys for the petty cash.

Even whilst all this was going on I somehow remained very good at my job. What I'd do was, I'd hide my problems all week acting like everything was ok to keep the punters happy and then at the weekends I'd push my emotions away or drown them out with drugs and drink so I didn't have to deal with them. This wasn't a very good way to handle things I know but it's all I could do at the time to keep my head above water.

I loved my job and all the attention and praise it was getting me. Being in front of a packed house every night and performing live and having to think on your feet was what I lived for but I couldn't keep up living this double life for long and the pressure of owing money and lying about my movements began to affect my performance. My problematic private life started to bleed into my public persona and people were noticing my erratic behaviour. I tried with all my might to keep it together but to add to my trouble I had now found ways of betting in the ship casino without getting caught. I'd build up a rapport with a gambling passenger and get him to place bets for me. I was still losing hand over fist though and in my desperation I managed to persuade Marco to advance me a whole month's wages ready for my next time ashore.

I was like a man possessed I couldn't wait to get to the bookies and, hopefully, recoup some of my losses. When I eventually did get there my first couple of bets went down and I was as glum as ever. There had to be more to life than losing all the f***ing time. Then my luck changed and bet after bet, my horses began winning. I couldn't believe it. I had pockets full of money and everything I touched turned into cold hard cash. I stayed in there until the shop closed and then made my way back to the ship not even knowing how much I'd won. I didn't want to check it in the bookies in case someone followed me out.

Back in my cabin I counted out my winnings. "F**k me! Three thousand pounds!" I hadn't seen that kind of money for ages. I was well chuffed and over the next two weeks was as happy as Larry. I spent hours daydreaming about how the money was going to change my life and what I was going to spend it on. I didn't have to pay back my wages as I could work them off and at last I felt like I had a bit of security. Even if I lost my job now it wouldn't matter as I had money and wouldn't have to live rough anymore. "Life on the open waves da da da da da da da da" I sang as I went to reception to let the old dears know that it was time for bingo.

I was getting well known by passengers and staff alike for my humour although I had been reprimanded by the Captain a couple of times for saying things over the ships intercom that upset some of the passengers. Miserable old gits.

One time I had gone to announce the bingo as normal but I was feeling rather cheeky and in a playful mood. I announced in a very serious voice, "Ladies and gentlemen could I have your attention please. This is a very important announcement. Could you please put down everything you are doing and listen very carefully..." Then after a long pause

I continued in a cheesy DJ voice, "It's time for bingo!" I laughed out loud but not everyone was amused and it was only a matter of minutes before the complaints began to come in. Apparently, some of the older folk thought the ship was going down and were having heart problems so I got severely reprimanded and told not to do it again. They even went as far as banning me from playing the theme from Titanic after the bingo. Amazing! Some people just can't take a joke. I didn't care though; I was always looking for other ways to relieve the boredom. It was time for me to go ashore again and with my new found confidence and luck I took up my usual activities and spent the first day and night getting p***ed and doing coke. Then on the Saturday I ventured out to the bookies, convinced it was going to be a repeat of last time, surely I was on a roll. I was sorely mistaken. My first few bets were quite large and lost so I started chasing my money again and upped the stakes. A big mistake.

I was down to one thousand out of the three I came in with and in a stupid blind desperate attempt to recoup my losses I put the whole lot on one horse. "And they're off…" said the American commentator as the horses left the stalls. All the British racing had long since finished and I was now betting on horses in Philadelphia. It was total madness; there was nothing in the papers about these horses. No form, no indication whatsoever. You had to go on the betting alone. Blind.

My horse was the favourite at odds of 4/5 which means it was supposed to be good and for every five hundred pounds I put on, I would get four hundred profit back if it won. My heart was beating like an express train. "They're coming round the final bend…" screamed the commentator. Mine was in front by a long way. "What's this?" he said. "Number 9 has come from way back and is now within one length of the leader. It's neck and neck as they come up to the line… Photo!" he shouted.

What? Oh, f**k! Where did that come from? I said to the only two other punters in the shop who were as stunned as I was, and they hadn't even had a bet themselves, they'd only stayed in the bookies to see if my huge gamble was gonna pay off. "Now, here come the results" came the voice over the speakers. The place went quiet and I took a deep breath hoping for a winning result. "In first place is … number 9, second number 1, and third number 6," came the result. "F***ing b***ard," I shouted angrily through clenched teeth letting out an enormous sigh and slamming my fist down hard on the counter.

I was a right miserable sod over the next few days and started feeling depressed and exasperated with myself. I really needed help from somewhere but was too proud to ask for it. Later that week I got chatting with a group of lads who had come on board and, feeling low, I let my guard down after they kept asking me if I'd like a drink. I gave in to temptation and allowed them to sneak me alcohol from the bar. I felt guilty at first but after the first few went down I didn't give a s**t and started on the doubles.

I always took things too far and started getting really loud and lairy and ended up in an argument with one of the passengers because I snogged his drunken girlfriend. Unfortunately he had a couple of mates with him and they kicked off causing a right scene. Someone went to reception and made a complaint about me to the ships bursar. Thankfully we got on really well and he sorted it out, locking one of the guys in the cells over night and sending me to my cabin.

The next morning I was woken up by someone banging on my door. "F**k off!" It didn't stop so, feeling like crap I got up and answered it. I didn't recognise the chap although he was dressed in ships uniform and looked official "Jonathan, the captain wants to see you in one hour", he said and walked off. Shit! I knew what that meant, breath test! I got some breakfast and tried to sober myself up.

I had a shower and some breakfast but by now fifty minutes had passed and I was bricking it. Marco was on leave so I had no one to talk to leaving me alone with my own thoughts, which was never a good thing. I knocked on the captain's door.

"Come," a stern voice called out. I went inside and was told to sit. The captain was only a little guy and had a bright red face like a slapped arse. It was set in permanent stare mode and he looked like he had never laughed in his life. He wore a crisp, well-ironed uniform and there was a strange looking contraption on his desk. It wasn't the first time I had been hauled into someone's office to be disciplined but this time he had the power to take away the only home I'd got and that worried me.

"You know why you are here Jonathan so let's just get on with it," he said matter of factly picking up the strange contraption which was obviously a breath test machine.

"This maybe an old breathalyser, but, nevertheless it works," he said.

"Oh s**t here we go," I thought having flash backs to when I got done for drink driving. I blew into it hoping it wouldn't expose my binge the night before but by the look on the captain's face I knew it was bad news.

"There is no doubt that you have been drinking Jonathan so I have no alternative other than to tell you to leave the ship as soon as we dock. You may go," he said, not even giving me a chance to plead for my job. I became angry and couldn't hold my tongue. "B****cks to you then," I told him as I stormed out slamming the door. I was in shock. I'd lost my job and my home and I had no money thanks to my gambling yet again, and all I had was half an hour to get my s**t together before we docked.

I packed what I could and left the rest of my stuff on board. I managed to sell my DVD player to one of the crew for fifty quid so at least I had a bit of money. I was good at packing things in a hurry and made short work of it. As I got off the ship, Marco was getting on and I had to tell him what had happened. He was devastated and to be honest I felt like I'd really let him down (sorry Marco).

As I walked away I turned round and took one last look at the ship shaking my head in disbelief. It had all happened so quickly, my arse didn't have time to touch the ground. There was no point getting all upset now. I turned away and headed off towards the train station. I had no idea where I was going. Once again, I was up s**t creek without a paddle and as the enormity of what had just happened began to dawn on me; I became overwhelmed and began to weep.

22
Bingo

I was now on the train heading back to Leicester and I called Kate on her mobile not knowing who else I could turn to. I could tell by the ring tone that she was abroad, probably in Hong Kong again. I was having all sorts of crazy ideas. I was thinking of breaking into her house while she was away, at least it would give me some time to get myself sorted out.

By the time I got there it was late evening and having lived there before I knew how to get into the house without causing any noticeable damage. I took a chance that if the neighbours saw me they wouldn't think anything of it as I had done it many times before. About ten minutes later I was in without any problems and as I had expected there was no one in. All her clothes were strewn everywhere so I presumed I was right about her being abroad as well. I lay in bed feeling guilty for being in her house without her consent but I had no other choice, it was a matter of survival. All I could do was think about what a s**ty day I'd had and how tired I was. It wasn't long before I fell asleep.

The next day I just chilled out, not having to entertain a ship full of people was great and all I wanted to do was drown my sorrows and have a holiday from myself. It was hard work being me, getting into trouble all the time and then having to patch up what was left of a seriously f***ed up life. I knew at some point Kate would be back so I decided to play on her kindness and called her telling her all the stuff that had happened to me and that I had nowhere to go so I'd broken into her house. It was a long shot as I'd given her nothing but trouble during our relationship but what did I have to lose? I called her and after a heated discussion she agreed I could stay there until she got back in two days time. I knew that this was a real lifeline and the fact she allowed me to stay gave me encouragement, that when she returned I might be able to persuade her to extend the offer to couple of weeks.

I was sat watching TV when she pulled up outside. She came through the door and looked at me in disgust. "You can't stay here," she said with sadness and anger in her voice.

"I've got nowhere else to go," I replied. We had a long talk, most of it arguing and in the end she agreed I could stay there as long as I left within a few days. The atmosphere was dire and we hardly spoke over the next twenty-four hours and when we did it was because we had to.

I started looking through the yellow pages for different hostels in Leicester and called several without any joy. Then I came across Kennedy House in South Wigston. Bingo! They had a vacancy and after chatting with a staff member I was asked if I would like to go down for an interview.

The hostel looked ok and to be honest, being at Kate's house was a nightmare. We just weren't getting on and the pressure was building by the second. I knew that this time Kate was serious about kicking me out. She seemed really bitter towards me and I didn't blame her, what with all the drugs, gambling and booze I'd done during our time together. She must have felt robbed of the guy she had once met.

It was awful. When I was finally accepted into the hostel. Kate took me down there crying her eyes out. I just did what I always did and looked for someone else to blame. I had a right go at her making her feel like s**t for not allowing me to stay and when I lost it, I lost it big time and could say things that were so evil and horrible that I could and did reduce many people to tears.

She left and sped off down the road and I didn't see her again for a long time.

That day something snapped inside of me. I started behaving in an even more erratic way and I saw a side to me that scared me. The negative evil thoughts in my head started to take over my personality and I truly felt that this was the beginning of the end.

23

Choices

I blacked out on a regular basis over the next few weeks as I began to drink like never before. The poison of choice this time was White Lightning cider. This stuff was lethal and drinking about six litres a day I would regularly get into fights with the other residents making a name for myself very quickly. One night after shouting abuse at anyone in earshot whilst drunk, I spilt cider all over a table in the communal lounge, and then went to bed to sleep it off. The next day after waking up feeling like s**t, I went back into the front room where I had been drinking and to my surprise and horror, the cider I had spilt had taken the top layer of varnish off the table. That's how minging this stuff was. On the label it says cider, but it tasted like the contents had never seen an apple before in its life. As I could never remember what had happened the night before, the next day I would treat everyone like they were my friends. It must have looked like I had a personality disorder. In some ways I think I did. I was seeing the CPN (Community Psychiatric Nurse) once a week and thought we were making progress, it was the first time in my life I had admitted I'd got a problem and actually wanted to do something about it.

Even though things on that front were looking up, I couldn't stop drinking and now a new lad with a serious heroin problem called Tam had moved in the hostel from Scotland. We got on really well at first and started hanging around together. Most of the time I was out of money due to my gambling which often left me without any alcohol. If I ran out of that I became depressed very quickly and in my desperation would reach for the nearest substitute and at that particular time, because Tam had a constant supply, the next best thing was heroin. I pestered Tam into giving me some and started trying a little bit at a time, not a lot, just a few tokes on the foil. To smoke heroin you would use two pieces of foil, one as a sort of pipe and the other to hold the brown (heroin) on as you chased it up and down the foil in lines. I didn't feel much of anything at first maybe a little bit stoned what with all the booze, medication and God knows what else whizzing around my body, I was surprised I felt anything at all.

Anyway whatever I felt, I knew I didn't like it and after a few days of trying it, and remembering the words 'you'll be instantly addicted for life' from years before, I started to crack up. I woke the next day feeling like s**t. I was shaking and sweating and not really sure what was happening but I knew that I was afraid of who I was becoming. My stomach was giving me serious trouble "Oh no, f**k!" I shouted, as the cramps started again. I just made it to the loo in time. I had chronic diarrhoea and sat there feeling sick in so many ways.

My mind was f***ed, my body was a mess and I'd been using heroin. I sat there in the dark with tears running down my face. What was I going to do? I was killing myself and it seemed I could do nothing about it. I was feeling so vulnerable, not in fear of anyone else, but in fear of what I might do to myself which was worse as I had absolutely no self control. I couldn't take much more.

I can remember praying and asking God to help me at that particular time, as I was so frightened of where I was heading. I prayed that God would not let me get addicted to heroin and in return I promised I would try to be a better person.

I didn't think I had the capability of actually honouring that promise but in my heart I'd meant it when I said I wanted to change and hoped that there was someone up there listening to me that would come to my rescue. I was still drinking hard over the next few weeks but I didn't touch heroin again. In an attempt to keep my promise I started to write down positive comments and put them on my wall, trying to encourage myself. Stuff like "You are the result of the choices you have made to date" and when I read these words it did two things. It showed me that the mess I was in was caused by the decisions I had made and showed me that if I began making the right decisions my life would bear the fruit of those right choices and I liked the idea of that. It doesn't seem that profound now but at the time those words struck a chord in me and even though the words couldn't change me themselves, they were pointing me to a better life but at the time I had no idea how to get there.

There were a few blokes in my block and we all shared a front room and two bathrooms. Most of them kept themselves away from me because I was unpredictable and volatile and soon after Tam moved out a couple of new fellas moved in. One was called Shane and the other was Donnie. Shane was about five eleven with a skinhead and loads of tattoos. Donnie was about five two, sixty years old and looked like a throw back from the fifties. He was a real pain in the arse and he could bu***hit for England.

Shane and I got on well from the start and would go out boozing together in the centre of Wigston, where we went to a Karaoke on a regular basis. Donnie would often follow us down there.

As we all lived in such close quarters, when we were in between Giros we would borrow money off each other when skint paying it back when we could. One particular day a new resident came round our block scrounging for tobacco, his name was Rob. He was tall and quite well built with a scar across his face like he had been slashed, but instead of knocking politely and waiting to be asked in he kicked the door open and barged into the hallway demanding a cigarette off Donnie.

He didn't see me sat in the front room and started gobbing off threatening Donnie and talking all kinds of crap. He clearly thought he could intimidate people and if there was one thing that wound me up, it was bullying. I'd quickly had enough of his s**t and jumped up out of my chair grabbed him round the throat and knocked him back out the front door. It must have hurt him as he looked totally disorientated and couldn't really talk. I was so angry and wanted to smash his face in but I was afraid of how far I might go. Bizarrely and luckily for him, I pressed the panic alarm near the front door and staff came running in. I was on edge at the time and could see myself seriously hurting the guy and doing time for it. I wasn't going to let that happen again.

When staff arrived I told them my version of events and because he'd had so much to drink they believed my story over his and he got kicked out. Things calmed down for the rest of the day and Donnie couldn't do enough for me.

The next night I asked Donnie to lend me four quid to get some White Lightning and he agreed. He'd been paid earlier that day. He said he'd be back around teatime to give me the cash but when he didn't turn up I remembered it was Karaoke night. I knew he would be down there as he fancied himself as a bit of a singer. I decided to pay him a visit and went down there to confront him.

Donnie must have seen me coming through the side window and did a runner out the back exit before I even set foot into the building. When I got in there and asked for him the Landlord told me he'd legged it only moments before. "The little s**t!" I shouted and in a rage ran out the pub to collar him. I saw him down the road and ran up to him shouting "Why you avoiding me?"

"I'm not," he stuttered back.

"Don't f***ing lie to me you s**t head." I screamed, grabbing his jacket and slapping him round the face. "Where's my money you b***ard?" I said spiting in his face. I'd lost the plot completely. Passers by were standing around watching the whole thing unfold and it was only when I noticed them I realised what I was doing and let him go. There were people all down the street, some going to the shops and others walking their dogs, all looking at me in disgust. What was I doing? I was behaving just like a bully myself.

I walked back to the pub to try and get away from the scene. Donnie had run off up the road saying he was going to call the police and I knew he wasn't lying.

I went into the pub and someone bought me a beer. I'd barely had a sip when the police arrived in full force, riot vans and everything.

I knew they'd come for me and didn't put up any resistance. There wasn't any point. I was guilty and didn't try and deny what I had done much to their relief. I was arrested and charged, then banged up for the rest of the night and released around 3 am. It was quite uneventful really. I didn't bat an eyelid as I'd been arrested so many times before. I went back to the hostel and got into bed thinking that was the end of that.

I found it hard to sleep that night and was desperate to break free from the torment I kept putting myself through. My mind overly active as normal was replaying images of bad things I'd done in the past and events that were long gone. It just wouldn't stop, it seemed endless and I couldn't get any peace.

There was a massive banging on my bedroom door and it sounded like someone was going to come crashing through it any minute.

I was half-asleep but woke quickly. As I answered the door I could see a load of coppers outside my window.

"What have I done now?"

"Just open up Jonathan," came the reply.

I was escorted down to reception and taken into the manager's office.

Her name was Margaret, she'd never liked me and I wasn't keen on her either.

"Jonathan," she said, "I was informed this morning that you assaulted one of our residents last night."

"Yeah, but it wasn't here. It had nothing to do with this place." I said, trying to defend myself aggressively knowing what was coming next.

"That's beside the point," she replied, "considering the circumstances and the fact that many residents have complained about you over the past few months due to your intimidating behaviour, I am left with no alternative other than to ask you to leave." I was fuming,

"You bitch!" I grunted at her.

The coppers heard my comments and one of them peered through the door of the office.

"Everything alright?" he asked.

"Yes, fine thank you. I was just telling Jonathan that he's got to be gone in fifteen minutes," she replied.

"Ok Jonathan?" said the copper.

"No I'm not f***ing ok, what do you think?" I snapped back.

"Listen, this can be easy or hard, it's up to you?" he said. "Just go and get your stuff and leave quietly and you won't end up getting nicked will you."

"Whatever," I shouted, storming off down the corridor to my room with the old bill in hot pursuit.

I packed whatever I could into a rucksack with the coppers standing over me watching.

"I can't believe this s**t!" I muttered under my breath. "Come on hurry up," said one of the pigs. I stood up and looked at him in the face and for a second was going to smash him in the gob but somehow managed to stop myself. Instead I shook my head at him with a look that could kill. "Out of my way then," I said in frustration, barging past one of them in the doorway. They followed me back to reception where I was told the rest of my stuff would be put into storage for three months and then disposed of if I hadn't collected it by then.

"Well, f**k you very much!" I yelled with venom at Margaret "Oh yeah, and I hope you have a nice tea tonight when you're back in your nice warm home and have a great Christmas won't you. Don't worry about me sleeping rough in the cold, which you could have stopped." She just stood there not knowing what to say as I stormed out yelling "Merry Christmas bitch!"

24

Hangover from hell

It was late November and the leaves had fallen from the trees spreading autumnal colours over the grass outside the hostel. It was a beautiful day but all I could see was the red mist of my anger. As I walked off towards the city I was dreading the prospect of another Christmas alone on the streets. I couldn't take much more of this. This isn't the way it was supposed to be I didn't want to be destined to a life of misery.

It seemed like a really long walk into town and when I got there I had no idea where to go. I'd burnt all bridges with anyone I knew in the city, through either not repaying borrowed money, drug related crime or just simply because I was a lying, cheating, deceitful git. Let's face it that's what I'd become. I felt that no one liked me or trusted me anymore. I wasn't wrong.

I soon found living rough again was driving me deeper in to a darkness that I might never recover from and I was regularly stealing just to keep my head above water. I knew I had to get into a hostel soon but the only one that would take me in was the Leicester night shelter.

That place was for the lowest of the low; you were scraping the bottom of the barrel if you had to go in there but right now I had no other choice. Beggars can't be choosers. It was made up of about thirty rooms with mostly blokes and if you were lucky you would only be sharing with one of them.

When I went in I was put in a room with three heroin users and these guys were leaving needles all over the place. If you got up in the middle of the night to go for a p**s it was a lottery as to whether you got stabbed in the foot by one.

Being in that environment sent me plummeting lower than I thought

I could ever go. No longer was I just thinking of ways to get out of the hostel but now I was thinking of how to get out of this misery altogether! I tried to keep those thoughts at bay as best I could, it was a slippery slope. Things were bad but it was still marginally better than being out on the streets. It was now winter and all the hardened homeless guys were coming in off the streets to escape the cold. As a result, there was a flood of new residents filling every empty space in almost every hostel throughout the Midlands. I didn't want to stay in the night shelter long and was phoning round everyday to all the listed hostels trying to get a room. What made it harder staying at the night shelter was the fact you weren't guaranteed a room every day, it was first come first served. You were kicked out with your bags every morning and then you had to be back by one o'clock in the afternoon to claim your bed or it was given to someone else.

As with all hostels there were a few lairy people in there with big gobs and I was getting fed up of hearing their voices. They would just pick on people for no apparent reason and I hated bullies. I'd come close to blows with one of them a couple of times before. I tried to keep myself clean and reasonably presentable and at first they thought I was an undercover copper. I had to convince them that I was the same as them and hated the old bill myself.

This took some doing and the regular big mouths would give me the odd dig during meal times, calling me 'pig'! Until one day I'd had enough.

"Listen you f***ing p**ck," I exploded. "I'm not a f***ing pig alright? And if I hear you mention it again I'll rip your f***ing head off do you understand?" I was seething, "And that goes for everyone else ok?" The whole place went quiet. Nobody bothered me after that, in fact people started to be nice to me, which was good. I was so angry I was almost at breaking point.

Eventually I found a room in 'Wordsworth Road Hostel' at the other end of town and moved out of the night shelter. It consisted of two houses joined together and an office for staff on the side. The houses were quite pleasantly decorated and it was the closest I'd come to a normal living environment for some time. There were about eight residents in all, four in my house and four in the other. The staff only worked until six o'clock and there was no security on in the evening making you almost feel like a real person. You could make your own meals and no one really bothered you, it was fantastic! Things were looking up. I settled in nicely and became good buddies with one of the residents called Ronnie. We were very much alike in many ways; he was about the same build as me only with short dark hair and he had a serious crack addiction. Still, he was very articulate and had a certain charisma about him similar to myself. It wasn't long before we were out robbing places and selling the stuff on, trying to make enough money each day to feed our habits one way or another. It was more lucrative for us to hang around together than to go it alone. And because we were so alike, opinionated, stubborn, and of course, always right, we had the odd argument or two but it never lasted long and we soon made up again.

I hadn't been there long, maybe a couple of weeks, when someone nicked the TV from the communal lounge and sold it to get drugs. I wasn't even in at the time but because I was the newbie the other guys told staff that it was me. Of course, they couldn't prove it but the staff were so convinced by the other residents that when I returned I was asked to leave.

"What the f**k?" I shouted, "I'm not going anywhere," I said defiantly.

"Well if you don't go, we will have to call the police," said the manager.

F***ing hell! Not this s**t again! I didn't know what to do. I had just got back from an extremely heavy night, doing goodness knows how much coke and with a hangover from hell. The last thing I needed right now was to pack my stuff and move on again. All I wanted to do was go to bed and sleep it off. This was f***ing crazy. I'd done nothing wrong. For once I was telling the truth but it made no difference. The manager motioned to the phone threatening to dial 999 so I just gave up.

"Ok, f**k you then, you bunch of w***ers!" I yelled marching to my room to get my things once again.

By this time it was almost Christmas and due to my drink and drug binge the night before I was completely skint. I quickly stuffed my belongings into a holdall and feeling weak, I went downstairs and was given my five pounds key deposit back that I'd paid when I moved in. I left in silence, unlike the last time just weeks before. I didn't have the energy to shout at the staff anyway. All my anger and frustration had turned into sadness and despair and feeling suicidal I slipped off into the cold night air.

25

Nelson Mandela

F**k this s**ty life! I walked back into town homeless again. It was about 10:30 at night, there was nowhere to go and that night was a cold one. I spent most of it walking around trying to keep warm and ended up sleeping under a bush in Saffron Lane Park covered in leaves. I didn't sleep much that night and was woken in the morning when an early riser's dog found me in the under growth.

"P**s off!" I growled, lashing out at the dog and scaring it off. I sat up quickly and just about managed to stop myself from peeing in my pants. That would have been the cherry on the cake on a cold day like this, walking round town with frozen beer p**s stains all over my trousers. I could see my breath in the morning air and decided to get up. My back was killing me and after quickly looking around to see if the coast was clear, I went for a slash against the bush that had sheltered me during the night. Usually it was not a good idea to p*** on your own doorstep but then I remembered I'd done exactly that only weeks before at Kennedy House. Steam rose up from my pee filling my nostrils with the smell of Sugar Puffs. It always smelt like that when I was dehydrated and reminded me that I hadn't eaten for about twenty-four hours. I gathered my things and got my s**t together and headed off towards town. I still had a couple of quid on me from the key deposit and was in need of some grub. McDonalds seemed like the best place. I could use their bogs to clean up and have a quick wash.

The Clock Tower struck nine and with a belly full of fast food I made my way to the council offices to try and secure a room. I didn't fancy sleeping out in that again. I was first in the queue. I took a ticket then sat down and waited for my number to come up. The room started to fill up with people in a similar position. I wondered what sort of chance

I had if all these people were here after the same thing.

"Ticket number one to room two please," said an automated voice from the speaker. I got up and went in. The room was small with a dividing partition across the middle and a large thick glass screen in the centre. There was a chair on each side of the screen. I sat down. After a couple of minutes a lady came through a door on the other side and sat down. She was short and plump with a round, soft looking face and rosy cheeks. She could have easily been Santa's wife.

"Can I help you?" she said.

"I hope so or I'm in the s**t," I replied, hoping that she'd have the miracle cure to solve my problems. I told her my situation and begged for her help and at first it looked good. She rustled some papers and left the office before returning for some more information. She spoke to different agencies about my situation but in the end, after waiting for a decision for two long hours, she came back and told me she was sorry but there was nothing they could do, as I wasn't classed as 'vulnerable enough'.

"Vulnerable! I am f***ing vulnerable. I feel like killing myself!" I replied angrily.

"Even so I'm afraid just feeling like it doesn't qualify you."

"What do I have to do to get help then, actually commit suicide?" I screamed in desperation. She looked at me with sad eyes and said,

"Well, yes. Those that have tried to take their own life do qualify and would fulfil the criteria needed to receive help." I couldn't believe what she was saying.

"Are you telling me that the only way you can help me is if I try and take my own life?" She didn't reply, I don't think she knew what to say. I sat there in silence, my mind feeling numb, completely stunned by what I'd just heard. I got up and left the building a broken man. Feeling like killing yourself wasn't taken seriously by the council, only when you had tried and failed would they take any real notice of you. I was up the creek without a paddle once again and felt I was left with no other choice.

I went to Nelson Mandela Park just off Welford Road and sat there drinking cider until nightfall. As the sun was setting it gave off a beautiful pink hue in the clouds and I sat on the bench staring at the sky finding comfort in the fact that there was something out there bigger than my troubles. Looking at the stars and moon made me feel strangely secure; they were so magnificent and eternal and usually gave me hope, but not tonight. I'd had enough and was crying out for help but there was only silence.

It seemed like nobody understood or wanted to understand what I was going through on the inside and I couldn't put up with the barrage of negative voices in my head anymore. My future looked none existent and the prospect of starting another year homeless was adding to my grief. The words of the lady in the council office earlier were repeating in my mind. F**k this s**t! In an act of utter desperation I took out my antidepressant tablets emptied the packet into my mouth and washed them down with cider.

For a few minutes I waited, set on dying. Then from somewhere deep inside, hope welled up in my heart. There had to be another way, I thought. A voice told me to get up and go to the hospital. Stumbling and snivelling, I struggled to my feet and made my way to A&E.

When I got there I couldn't go in. It was ridiculous. There I was over-dosed on tablets and I felt embarrassed because I'd done such a stupid thing. I stood outside thinking about what to do. By now I wasn't feeling at all well and was slumped against the wall. A nurse came over and asked me if I was ok. I was getting weaker by the minute.

"I need help, I've taken tablets," I slurred.

I don't remember much after that apart from coming round in a cubicle much later, with all sorts of wires stuck to my chest.

"You'll be ok," said a nurse, "the doctor will be back in a minute." I was really tired and must have been out for some time as it was now late evening. The doctor arrived and we talked about why I had taken an overdose and he reassured me everything was going to be alright.

While I was unconscious the doctor had called the Leicester night shelter and they had promised me a bed for the evening, something they didn't normally do but under advice from the doctor they made an exception. I must have told the nurse my story earlier on but couldn't remember doing it.

I wasn't sure if going back in the night shelter was good or bad thing but at that time I felt so ill I just wanted to get off the streets. Maybe now people would take me seriously when I said I couldn't take anymore, and give me the help I so desperately needed. After I'd been given the all clear I was taken down to the night shelter and booked in.

There weren't any beds available that night so I was put on a camp bed in the dining area until the morning. After that I'd be back to square one again, having to queue for a bed just like everyone else.

I was so tired that I couldn't even find the energy to think about the problems tomorrow would bring and after about an hour or so of tossing and turning, I finally fell asleep.

26

Jacket potato and tuna

I woke up early the next day and, although still groggy, got up and showered before anyone else surfaced. I had some breakfast and hung around for as long as I could until they threw everyone out at eleven am. That day was a bit of a blur. I spent most of it feeling desperately depressed, wandering around thinking about yesterday's events, questioning why I'd let myself go so low and wondering if I would ever try and top myself again. Did I have any control over it? I wasn't sure. By four o'clock that afternoon I was desperate for help and because I wasn't having any luck in Leicester, I decided to catch the bus to Loughborough to see if I fared any better there.

On the way over I started thinking about my mum who I hadn't contacted for ages. As soon as I got off the bus I gave her a call. I told her about everything that had been happening and she drove into town to meet me outside McDonalds. When she saw me she nearly cried. I looked awful. My face and hands were filthy, I had a week's stubble and my clothes were starting to smell.

"Hi mum," I said quietly.

"Oh Jonathan," she said, throwing her arms around me. "You look terrible. Come on let's get you sorted out." She took me down to the council offices to see if we could make an appointment with a housing officer. They were just closing up but two men came over to us and asked if we needed any help. The first guy was Asian, he was tall about six two and well built. The other guy was much shorter with a wispy moustache and both of them seemed genuinely caring types; they gave off a sort off warmth that made them easy to talk to. It turned out that they were both Christians. I don't remember their names but the shorter one was nick named 'Born again Len.' They were both really helpful and gave me and Mum some numbers of places to call that might take me in. There was nothing we could do that night as everywhere was closed so we'd have to make the calls the next day.

It was difficult for mum to put me up because she only had a one bedroom flat but nevertheless she did and I am grateful to her to this day for all of her help she gave me at the lowest point in my life.

I stayed at her flat over the following week until I eventually found a room in the East Midlands Hotel (EMH) which is a hostel for people on the council house waiting list. Thankfully I had family in the area and that entitled me to go on the list for a flat of my own.

The EMH was situated near the train station and was close enough to walk to town. The hostel itself used to be a thriving hotel at one point with quite a lively bar. I can remember drinking there years before but never would have thought I'd be back under such circumstances. It was made up of about sixty rooms and still had the layout of a hotel so they hadn't needed to do much work to change it over. To get to your room you had to press a buzzer then a staff member would let you in. You'd then go up to the reception desk and ask for your room key which you had to hand in each time you left the building. I had been put in room number seven which was conveniently downstairs. All rooms had an en suite bathroom and two single beds. It was very cosy. The staff seemed nice and for an extra pound a day you could have a full cooked breakfast between 7.30 and 9.00 if you could be bothered to get up in the morning.

The only downfall was the curfew they had in place. You had to be back in the hostel by midnight or you were locked out and could face eviction if it continued. By the time I got in there it was just before Christmas and my mum helped me settle in, giving me cutlery and some of the essentials to try and make it feel like home. I stayed in for the first few days, keeping a low profile and getting some much needed rest, but as each day went by Christmas got nearer and I started to venture out on the beer again, seeing old mates from years gone by and before long was doing a bit of Charlie as well. I was always amazed at how I managed go out with five quid and come home seven hours later with twenty quid in my pocket after drinking and doing cocaine all day. When I wanted money to go out I could be ruthless. I even went to my mums on Christmas Eve and begged her to give me some money to go out, resulting in a huge argument until she finally gave in and gave me her last ten pounds which I blew on beer (Sorry mum).

Christmas day was spent in my room eating a jacket potato and tuna and drinking wine supplied by one of the other residents, which helped me forget where I was. There seemed to be an endless flow of booze in the hostel even though you weren't allowed to drink in there. Christmas day passed much like any other really and by the time New Years Eve came round, I'd got to know quite a few people in the hostel and was invited out for a drink. I had a few quid left on me due to the fact that over the Christmas period you would receive two giros because the dole office would be closed into the New Year.

A few of us went out and I was having a great night. It was getting closer to midnight and I decided I'd stay out and see the New Year in, thinking they would make an exception with the curfew considering it was New Year's Eve. "Ten, nine, eight, seven" the countdown began and I was determined to start the year on a good note. There was a screen in the pub that showed the fireworks at Trafalgar Square as 2004 was welcomed in. The whole pub erupted in celebration. Blokes were snogging girls they didn't know, glasses were clinking everywhere and it seemed like a great end to a disastrous year. By this time I'd probably had about ten pints and was pretty drunk so I left the pub and stumbled back to the hostel.

It must be a miracle. I'd seen the New Year in and I wasn't actually homeless. Maybe this is a sign of things to come.

When I got back I found the doors had been locked and buzzed reception to let me in. Nobody responded the first time I buzzed so in my drunken stupor I just kept on buzzing until someone eventually came to answer. The security guard who was on shift that night was a large bloke of about 6 foot and wore the traditional security guard uniform of black trousers, highly polished boots, white shirt, black tie and black v neck jumper. You could tell by his body language that he took real pride in his job, knowing it gave him a certain power over those less fortunate than himself. He would look at you down his nose, through his handlebar moustache like a prison screw, making you feel like a piece of s**t that had somehow gotten on his shoe. He had never really liked me and when he came to the door he flatly refused to let me in, telling me, with great pleasure that I should have come back at the right time and as I hadn't, could now stay out all night. He could've easily have let me in but seemed determined to show off the little bit of authority he had and stood there with a smile on his face. Big mistake, as that just added fuel to the fire.

"Let me in you fat b****ard" I yelled, banging hard on the door which was probably not the best way to get him to let me in.

"You're definitely not coming in now," he hissed at me.

"F**k you then and happy New Year," I bellowed back at him.

I went round the back of the building and made several attempts to break in but was unsuccessful. All I wanted was to get my head down and that power crazy t**t wouldn't let me in. By this point I was shouting abuse at the top of my voice so he called the pigs. Within a flash they arrived and arrested me for being drunk and disorderly and carted me off to the cells, much to the amusement of the security guard.

The ten pints I had had earlier were in full effect and I was so p***ed I couldn't cause the old bill much bother and spent a relatively quiet night in the cells. In the morning I was released without charge and as I left, the sergeant on duty said with a smile "Johnny be good today eh."

"Whatever," I said back.

It was the first of January 2004 and I had started the year off in a f***ing police cell. I headed back to the hostel. Maybe if I went back and apologised they'd give me another chance. When I got there I found my stuff had already been put in black bin bags and left by the front door. I tried to talk to the manager on duty but was basically told to sling my hook. It turns out that the security guard was the manager's husband and had gone home that night and told his wife about my exploits, thus sealing my fate. By this time I was feeling seriously dehydrated and hung over. On top of that was the fact that I was once again homeless, with no money and no where to go. "F***ing hell!" I screamed at the top of my voice, picking my bags up and walking off in a huff. When would this s**t end?

I can't even remember where I stayed that night but do remember the following day. I was so p***ed off with being homeless again I went straight to the council office, sat in the middle of the floor with my bags and shouted that I was not moving until I was housed. There weren't many people in there but everyone heard me including all the staff, which was what I wanted. They tried asking me to move but I refused so they sent for security. A few minutes later a great big, black, security guard came over to me and asked me to leave.

"If you f***ing touch me I'll smack you one," I told him expecting a struggle, but his reaction took me by surprise and instead of grabbing me and throwing me out, he bent down quite gently putting himself at my level and asked me what the problem was.

"I'll tell you what the problem is mate," I said in a much quieter voice, trying to hold back the tears. Then I explained to him what had happened to me over the past few days and months.

"Oh dear," he said sincerely, "you have had a rough time haven't you? Just wait here and let me go and have a word with the housing officer." I let out a huge sigh. Maybe now someone will listen to me.

The security guard disappeared into a room and I sat waiting for an answer. Things never moved quickly when you were dealing with the council and after a while my bum started hurting from the hard floor. So, because I'd made my point, I decided to take the more comfortable approach and sat in one of the chairs provided.

I was really tired and was almost asleep when I heard my name called.

"Jonathan Kinch?" said the lady behind the counter. I jumped up and went over frowning, expecting an argument.

"We have got you into the King's Head Hotel in Kegworth," she said. "It isn't a hostel but they do allow people on benefits to stay there from time to time and have agreed to give you a chance."

I dropped my head back in relief. "Thank you so much," I said with a lump in my throat.

I couldn't believe my luck. Things had never happened this fast before but I wasn't about to complain all I wanted was to go to bed and sleep for ages.

"How am I going to get there?" I asked.

"We will even give you the bus fare," she said.

"Oh thank you," I said, feeling a bit awkward and embarrassed about what I'd had to do to get listened to. I was asked to sign some paperwork, fill out the relevant housing benefit documents and then I was on my way.

I caught the bus from town and sat back in the seat letting my body relax for the first time in ages. As the bus left town I closed my eyes and thanked God that I'd got somewhere to stay. It was a poor start but maybe this year would turn out alright after all.

27
Puke

My room was quite small and in the basement. The décor was green and blue striped wallpaper, which was minging, but it had all the things I needed to get by. There were two single beds, a small TV and a shower but no central heating. Thankfully there was a small electric heater that just about managed to take the chill out of the air. There was a communal kitchen for me to use and as the freezers were always full with hotel food, I just helped myself and nobody seemed to notice. By now I was on the housing list and knew it was only a matter of time before something came up. All I needed to do was hang in there and not get evicted and I stood a good chance of sorting myself out.

As the days went by I began to get concerned about my forthcoming court cases. One was for slapping and spitting at Donnie which had resulted in me being kicked out of Kennedy House Hostel and the other was for a more serious case. In the short time I was living at Wordsworth Road Hostel I had been arrested for assault and criminal damage.

It all happened one night when I was out on the lash in town. After consuming a large amount of alcohol and mixing my drinks I went for the customary chicken and chips to take home and eat in bed. Everything was going fine, I'd got my grub and hailed a black cab (except these were yellow) to take me home. The journey was going well but after a few minutes I started feeling sick and threw up. It wasn't much but enough for the driver to notice. The driver was about 40 years old and much like many other taxi drivers in Leicester was foreign.

"You alright mate?" He said.

"Yeah I'm fine" I slurred back at him. We pulled up outside the hostel and I offered him the fare as he put the interior lights on to see if there was any puke in the back. There was a small amount on the floor but nothing that couldn't be sorted; as soon as he saw it he became very angry, demanding I pay him twenty-five quid as a clean up charge. There was no way I was paying twenty five quid when I could go inside, get a cloth and clean it myself for free. He was having none of it and locked the doors so I couldn't get out. I was trapped in the back seat with a Perspex screen separating me from the driver. I was pretty close to home but was now being held in his cab like a prisoner.

"Come on mate," I yelled at him. "Open the door!" but he ignored me and drove off.

"I'm taking you to police…" he shouted, "…then you pay fare." He was basically saying I wouldn't pay but the truth was when we had arrived outside the hostel I'd offered to pay him but he refused. This got me really angry and I went mad exploding into a torrent of abuse.

"Pull over you piece of s**t!" I screamed, but he didn't respond and was now driving at high speed swerving in and out of the traffic. I wasn't wearing any seat belt and as he braked sharply to avoid a collision I was propelled forward, bashing my head on the Perspex screen.

"You f***ing b****rd," I yelled. By this time I'd had enough and started whacking the screen with my fist until it smashed allowing me to get my arm through. I pulled his hair and hit him in the head and face trying to make him pull over. The car was bouncing all over the place and we were approaching town fast. As we pulled round the corner there was a police car sat in the layby. The cabby drove straight over and screeched to a halt in front of the coppers jumping out and waving his arms in hysteria. He told the police his version of what had happened while I was still locked in the back of the cab with cuts to my hands and covered in chicken and chips. The coppers came to the side of the cab and talked to me through the window, I cant tell you what they looked like as I was so p***ed I can't remember, but they were just making sure I was calm enough to be let out.

"What's your name?" one asked.

"Johnny Kinch…" I said, suddenly sobering up "…and I'm fine so just let me out". He looked at me then looked at the cabby.

"Look, it's that mad t**t you want not me," I protested. "You should be arresting him, he wouldn't let me out the cab."

"Have you had anything to drink sir?" said one of them.

"I've had a couple," I replied.

"Right we're going to open the door and let you out so you'd better behave yourself ok?" said the other one.

"Alright," I said.

They let me out then one of them took a look inside and saw the damage to the partition window confirming the cabbies story. Then, with no interest in my version of the event, he said, "Mr Kinch I'm arresting you on suspicion of…" Here we go again. I was put in cuffs, taken off to the cop shop and charged with assault and criminal damage before being released on bail the following day.

Anyway, that was a while ago and if I could get a flat before the court date there was a good chance I wouldn't be sent down.

I got up to all the usual stuff over the next few weeks, gambling, robbing, borrowing, begging, fighting, drinking and doing drugs as and when I could afford it. All the years of hard drinking etc were starting to catch up with me and I wasn't feeling too good. I had put an awful lot of weight on due to my erratic binge eating habits and had become extremely unfit. I desperately wanted to sort myself out but every time I wanted to do right I just did more wrong, but ever the optimist, I gave myself six months to get into shape if I got a flat.

I received a letter franked Charnwood Borough Council and knew that this would be the letter I'd been waiting for. I opened it. "Yes about f***ing time," I yelled. I had been offered a one bedroom flat slap-bang in the town centre. They had made me an appointment to go and see it in five days time and if I liked it, it was just a matter of signing the papers and getting the key. The following week I made my way to see the flat; it was on the third floor in a block on Russell Street.

The area was really rough, most of the drug dealers I knew lived there so it wasn't the most desirable location. As I walked to the downstairs door there was loads of rubbish outside. It looked like people had been dumping there for some time. I tried to see past it telling myself it was nothing that couldn't be sorted. When I got inside the hallway, I was greeted by graffiti all over the walls and foil, empty beer cans and loads of fag ends all over the floor.

It didn't look much better inside the flat either. The council had been in and ripped everything out and the place looked bare but I was desperate to get my own gaff and thought I could make it home with a little TLC. Besides if I started to get myself together the judge would look favourably on me and I might avoid prison. I went back to the council and told them I wanted to accept their offer and after signing a tenancy agreement was given the keys.

I couldn't believe it. On the 16th February 2004 I had my own flat. I had already applied for a community care grant some weeks earlier and the grant came through just after I moved in. I was all set; my plan was taking shape. I hurriedly opened the envelope to see how much I'd been awarded. Seven hundred quid! 'Ok don't blow it' I told myself. Thankfully I didn't have to worry about my rent as I was claiming housing benefit and I could concentrate on spending the money on much needed furniture. I started planning what I was going to get and in my excitement went for a drink in town. After all, I deserved it. Just a few pints and I'll get going.

I felt great. I had cashed the giro at the post office and had a pocket full of notes. The first few pints went down with ease and as I sat there looking around the pub I noticed a small TV over the bar showing the racing. At first I took no real interest but as the beers started going down, I became more interested and asked the barman to turn it up. They were showing the horses and jockeys parading and getting ready to race. Then the betting came up on screen.

"The favourite looks good today, surely he won't get beaten?" said the commentator. I had to agree with him, he did look good. F**k it, I'm having a bet! I left the pub and ran to the bookies across the road. I knew it was a bad idea and a voice inside told me not to do it but I ignored it. Once I had got it in my head that I would do something there was no stopping me.

Some hours later...

"Pint of lager please," I said depressed.

"What's up? You had a bad day?" asked the barmaid. I didn't even acknowledge her and drank my beer down in one. "Got a spare fag?" I asked a guy sat next to me. Things had gone terribly wrong again. I'd blown the lot. The whole seven hundred. As always, even though I'd started out with good intentions, I'd managed to f**k things up yet again. This wasn't a good start and the rest of that day and night was unbearable. At least I had a home to go to, I thought positively. I had big plans for the flat but now had no money or furniture. No settee, no fridge, no bed, nothing, and to add insult to injury I also had no heating or electricity, because like most council flats there was a prepayment meter fitted as the previous owner couldn't pay his bills either.

The next morning I didn't feeling too happy. I woke up with the sun shining in my eyes but in my head it felt like a dull rainy day. I had to pick myself up and dust myself down; getting all depressed wasn't going to get me anywhere. I had to make some money or at least get some furniture from somewhere and began racking my brain trying to think of anyone who could possibly help. Then it came to me. The Actors Benevolent Fund. They'll help me. All I needed was enough money for a phone call and I'm sure they'd help me out.

I don't know how I did it but within two weeks I had a new double bed, a fridge freezer and my whole flat had laminated flooring all thanks to the ABF. And it didn't stop there, I bumped into a bloke I knew and he said he'd received help from a local church when he'd moved and asked me if I would like him to get them to call me.

"Yeah," I said, and sure enough, just like he said within a day or so they called and brought round a sofa and some chairs. It was really nice of them, and even though I'd messed up, with the help of some kind folk my empty cold flat started to take shape and began to feel like a real home.

28

Oscar winning performance

My court case was only a few days away and I was getting slightly worried to say the least. I spent the weekend getting hammered just in case it was my last chance for a while, or at least that was my excuse! I didn't really have any smart clothes so I couldn't dress to impress the judge that following Monday so I just wore what I'd got and made my way down there hoping for the best.

In court things happened quite quickly and after the solicitors had gone through all the usual stuff, and me and the cabby I'd assaulted had testified, they retired to decide on their verdict. They didn't stay out long though. "Mr Kinch we find you guilty as charged blah, blah, blah". That was all I heard. F***ing hell. Now I was in deep s**t. Bail was granted and I was given another date in two weeks time to appear for sentencing but before this could happen I had to go for a pre-sentence report at the probation office. If I could get them to give the judge a good report I still had a chance of escaping prison.

The next two weeks seemed like hell waiting to find out what my fate was and I drank more than ever to blot out the feelings of desperation. I had slowed down on the cocaine front though, not out of desire but more the lack of funds. My gambling was still way out of control and had now become my biggest problem.

When the probation office had finished writing the report I was given a chance to read it. It was an honest enough appraisal but I didn't particularly like what I read, it certainly didn't boost my confidence about escaping a custodial sentence but there was naff all I could do about it.

When the date for my reappearance came round I was bricking it. I couldn't even entertain the thought that I might be going to prison again. That would be the nightmare scenario and I didn't think I'd cope, especially after last time.

I took my mum along as she was going to give evidence if needed about how I'd made an effort to change since I'd been given a flat. This was a real stretch of the imagination but I did appreciate the fact that she'd even bothered to come with me. I certainly didn't deserve any support.

We hadn't been there long when we were called into the courtroom. I was told to stand in the dock and my mother sat at the back.

The solicitors reminded the judge of all the facts in the case and reeled off all my previous convictions. And after listening to my lengthy previous record I felt it wasn't looking good. Then my solicitor asked the judge to listen to my mother's statement about how I had changed and how she was going to support me over the coming months. The judge consented to listen and my mum took the stand giving an Oscar winning performance, even impressing me. After that, the atmosphere changed in the room and for the first time in this case I felt hopeful.

"All rise" said the barrister, as the female judge went out to deliberate. A few moments passed then the door that the judge left through opened again. Mum looked over and smiled and I knew that this was it, make or break. Under my breath and in utter desperation I was uttering, "Please God help me out here."

"All rise" said the barrister again, as the judge returned. "Well Jonathan, somebody must like you" she said. "I'm going to give you one more chance, and this is only because of your mother's support, so you owe it all to her really. I'm going to give you a six month tagging order ok?" She said not asking, but telling me. To be honest I was hoping to just get a fine but it was better than prison so I said,

"That's great your honour."

I was then released and a date of 26th May was set for the tagging company to come out to the flat and fit my tag and box.

I was well chuffed with the result. I'd escaped a prison sentence and thanked mum profusely in the pub after as we celebrated with a couple of drinks. (Cheers Mum!)

I knew that that was a close one but on the way home in the car, I had already, stupidly, began thinking of ways to beat my curfew.

29
Nutter

The date for the tagging soon came round and that was that, I was now technically a prisoner in my own home. My orders were to be in by 7 pm every night and I wasn't allowed to leave my flat until after 7.00 am. I had never been one for staying in or going to bed early so being in by seven each night was going to be difficult, but I had no choice. For the first few nights it was a bit of a novelty, I was showing people my tag left, right and centre like it was an expensive piece of jewellery. I used to sell fake Tag Heuer watches and one guy commented that knowing me the tag on my ankle would probably be fake as well. By the weekend the beer was calling me and the novelty of stopping in was starting to wear off.

I couldn't bear it anymore and decided to go out. I had intended to be back before seven but after about six or seven pints and giving it large on the karaoke I thought,

F**k this, I'm staying out and got home at about two the next morning.

The tagging company (Premier) had installed a box that picked up the signal sent from my tag each time I went in or out of the flat so they knew exactly what time I'd got in. There was also a phone attached to the box that they would call from time to time to check all was well and to find out why you were late.

When I got back that morning, the phone started ringing immediately and because I was so p***ed and didn't have an excuse, I ignored it hoping they'd just forget about it. The next afternoon I was woken by the phone ringing again and knew that if I didn't answer it this time and give them a good reason for my absence, I'd be in trouble later down the line. Premier didn't call the police immediately if you were late, they'd allow you to be one or two minutes late occasionally but if it went over an hour in total you would be hauled back to court to explain why. I was seven hours over already and I'd only been tagged for a month, what possible excuse was I going to give?

I picked up the phone and a young lady spoke.

"Hello this is Premier Security; I'm just calling to check you are alright?" she said.

"Err yes I'm fine," I said nervously expecting the worse.

"Great, any problems just let us know," she said and then put the phone down.

Well, that wasn't what I expected. It was a big mistake on my part, as I took that brief conversation to mean they didn't care that I was not coming in on time, so that kind of behaviour continued on through the summer months. I was late by at least a couple of minutes just about every day. Sometimes I had to make up b***s**t stories to explain where I had been but nobody had come round and arrested me yet so I thought I'd got away with it.

I did stay in from time to time but the only thing that made it worth while was plenty of beer and if Big Brother was on TV. I didn't particularly like the program but I knew that they were locked in just like me and that made it easier somehow. I guess I was waiting for the show to end because I knew that by then I would only have a few weeks left as a housemate myself.

One night, I got really drunk, staying out until the early hours and because of all the s**t I'd been through over the last few years, I became emotional as it all caught up with me. I was convinced that this time if I didn't have a good excuse for staying out they'd definitely lock me up and I got it into my head that if I could get someone in a position of authority to vouch for my whereabouts then the tagging company would believe my story. I decided in my drunken stupor that if I hurt myself and was seen by a doctor in A&E that would do it. It was a stupid idea but I was so drunk it seemed like a master plan to me. I staggered down to the walk in centre in Loughborough and took a run with my head at the wall outside. There was a thud and I bounced off rubbing my ear. I'd lost my bottle right at the end of my run and slowed down before clipping my ear on the wall. Like an idiot I had another go. This time I ran a bit harder. BANG! I came round to see two paramedics standing over me; I'd knocked myself out.

"Are you alright mate?" one of them asked.

"Am I badly injured?" I asked hoping they would admit me thus giving me an alibi.

"No," he said "You've just got a graze on your forehead."

"Is that it?" I asked with disappointment. They must have thought I was a total nutter. I got up and went home feeling stupid and with a really sore head. As soon as I got in, Premier called and I gave them my story. They asked if I was ok and told me to rest. I couldn't believe such a company could be such suckers, presumably they'd believed my lies but all it had really proved was that I was the sucker!

30
Oh brother!

I realised I hadn't seen my mum for a couple of months and because I'd run out of gas I thought I'd go round and tap her up for a few quid. My mum only lived about ten minutes walk from me but when I got there she wasn't in so I called her mobile.

Little did I know but at the same time this was taking place, an old mate of mine Jonnie Cave, was looking for me. He'd become a Christian a couple of years earlier and whilst praying, felt that God wanted him to find me and tell me what had happened to him. He'd already spent his spare time over the past three weeks going round the bookies and looking in all the pubs for me but with no joy, but on this particular day he'd had enough and decided to go to Tesco's to get some food for lunch.

My mum's phone was now ringing and she answered sounding surprised to hear from me.

"Where are you?" I asked, telling her I was outside her flat.

"I'm in Tesco's," she answered, and having said that she walked straight in front of Jonnie Cave.

"Wow Pauline," he said "I've been looking for Johnny for ages, have you seen him?"

"I'm on the phone to him right now," she replied, "I'll call you back," she told me putting the phone down. After a brief chat she told him that I was outside her flat and he asked if he could go back with her to see me. They left the store and on her way back she called to tell me why she'd had to go and told me she had spoken to Jonnie Cave.

"Just wanted to let you know that when I was talking to Jonnie he told me he's become a Christian!" She said.

"What! You're joking!" I said.

You see, I'd known Jonnie for a long time and we'd done loads of naughty things together, cocaine, heavy drinking, crime, you name it. So me, knowing what I knew about him, made it very hard for me to take in what she'd just said. It would've been easier to believe he'd had a sex change. I mean that would have been drastic but as far as I could tell it's generally more common place and acceptable on TV in this day and age than becoming a Christian. I mean A CHRISTIAN!

What did he want to go and do something like that for?

Christians are weirdos. Well, that's what I thought and I was going to stick to it. To be honest I didn't know I felt so strongly about it.

He arrived outside my mums flat and got out of his car. He looked normal enough but then he opened his gob.

"Brother!" he said walking over to me and gave me a hug.

"Oh brother!" I thought.

We went inside and mum made us a drink. We chatted for a while and he seemed really happy. It wasn't long before he started telling me his story. "I was away on holiday with the lads in Gran Canaria when it all happened for me" he said. "And after a night out on the town I went back to my apartment and fell asleep..."

"Ok," I said, with raised eyebrows, dubious about what was coming next. You see, this guy in many ways was just as bad as I was. He was a serial womaniser, regular drug user and got into his fair share of fights. So as he was talking I was expecting Jeremy Beadle to jump out at any minute and say "Gotcha!" As he continued, I began to realise that something had happened that night which had changed his life forever. He went on, "...after falling into a deep sleep I began dreaming, but it was no ordinary dream," he said. "I was in, what seemed like heaven, and was overcome with a feeling of immense happiness and joy which could not be compared to any false, temporary feeling experienced in all of my years of doing drugs". He went on explaining that he now knew that it was the presence of God and it was amazing.

I didn't know where to look or what to say and felt embarrassed.

"I'm glad for you," I said in total disbelief.

"It was weird," he continued. "It was just like the Philadelphia advert," he said laughing. "Everyone was dressed in white and I felt totally at peace, something I'd never experienced before." I've got to admit I was quite shocked by his story. What made it weirder was he seemed to be on the level. Apart from me, I thought Jonnie would be the last person on earth to commit their life to God. I mean, what did he need God for? He was loaded! But here he was, larger than life, telling me he'd changed and I could too if I only believed. He went on to tell me that when he'd got back to the UK, he kept the whole thing a secret until it happened again six months later and by that time he couldn't hold it in anymore, telling his mum (Diane) the whole story. She was probably just as amazed as I was but strangely someone had called her just the day before and invited her to a Church service in the small mining town of Ibstock. As if by divine appointment Diane and Jonnie went along. That day a preacher spoke and as the message of salvation through Jesus Christ filled the air, Jonnie, once again, felt that same peace he'd felt during his dream months before. He decided to make a commitment, giving his life to Jesus. He went on to tell me that Jesus, as the Son of God, came to the earth to take away the sins of mankind and that he died as a sacrifice for those sins, only to rise again from the dead three days later. He said that if I believed in him, I too could have a new life.

That was all very well but how does that help me out of the s**t I'm in right now? Jonnie told me that he'd pray for me and would stay in touch if I wanted. I agreed and we exchanged 'phone numbers. As I watched him pull away I was gob smacked.

"I can't believe that mum. Who would have thought he would have turned into a God freak? Anyway..." I said changing the subject "...can you lend me a tenner?"

31

Knock knock

"Come on you donkey. Oh B******cks!" I yelled at the bookie's monitor screen. My horse had just lost and I'd blown my giro again for another two weeks. I left the bookies in a huff and went to the pub across the street. I managed to scrounge a pint off a geezer I knew in there. "What am I gonna do now?" I thought staring into a half-empty glass. As I went through possible people in my mind who might give me a loan, I thought of Jonnie, he's got loads of cash and what's more, he's a Christian so he couldn't refuse. I reckoned that if I could get round to his house I'd definitely get some money out of him. I necked the rest of my pint and went home to ask my neighbour if I could borrow his push bike to get there as Jonnie only lived a couple of miles away from me. I took some unpaid bills with me and concocted a story about how I desperately needed to pay them. Cycling like mad I got there in about ten minutes flat and when I pulled up outside his house his car was in the drive. He was in. I rang the doorbell and prepared myself for a bit of acting.

"Johnny Kinch how are you? Come in," he said. "What brings you here mate?" I sat down and he made us a cup of coffee. I didn't hold back and straight away told him about my problems. Even though the problems were real, my intentions were to spend whatever money I could get from him on other things. He seemed very sympathetic towards me and kept telling me the only way was, "To put my trust in Jesus" and said that if I was prepared to do that "He would show me how to sort all my problems out." I wasn't buying it and told him my problems were not imaginary but real and even if I made a commitment to "Jesus" (which I wouldn't) it wouldn't solve anything. I paced around the front room while he disappeared upstairs; I thought he'd gone to use the bathroom but when he came down he had something in his hand and, looking at me with kindness in his eyes he said,

"Johnny I want to help you and want you to know that God loves you." Then handed me an envelope full of cash. He'd only given me half his wage packet, hundreds of pounds! I didn't know what to say. Inside I was jumping for joy and at the same time felt guilty for stretching the truth and putting him in such a position. No matter how guilty I felt though, I wasn't going to turn it down.

"Thanks, that will really help," I said stuffing the money in my pocket.

"Promise you will pay your bills with it," he asked.

"Yeah, of course I will if I don't I'll lose my flat" I said as a convincer.

"Good, and will you do me a favour?" he asked.

"Yeah, sure," I said.

"Would you come with me to a church service just to see how it is?" I stood there thinking about it. I mean, how bad could it be? A load of old biddies and a load of religious types, I should be able to make a few quid.

"Yeah ok, I'll go," I said on reflection.

"Great, I'll pick you up on Sunday at nine forty five then." We said our goodbyes and I jumped on the bike and made my way back to town. I had no intention of paying my bills and to be honest it hadn't even crossed my mind. I headed straight for the bookies. (It didn't go well. Enough said)

I woke up on Sunday morning to the sound of Jonnie knocking at my door. I had a massive drink and drug hangover and had blown all the money he had given me so there was no way I was going to answer it and go to church with him. He kept on knocking. F*** me he was persistent, but after about ten minutes of non-stop knocking I heard him drive off in his car. I've got to admit I felt a bit guilty about not going; after all he had been my mate for years and had given me half his wage packet. I felt lousy from the drugs, booze and medication and strangely felt pretty bad conscience wise too. As I lay back down I couldn't help thinking of how I'd let him down. I took some pain killers with another drink and went back to sleep. As well as it playing on my mind, there was no getting away from him either; he called the next day asking where I'd been. I told him some cock and bull story, which, thankfully, I think he swallowed. He probably did know the truth but didn't want to let on. He asked if he could come round to see me the following day, I agreed but was afraid he might ask what I'd done with the money he'd given me. That day I went out and sold my mobile phone thinking I could use the money to win a few quid, at least I'd have something to show him when he came round, but as usual I lost the lot. I was going to have to lie to him again to cover my previous story. All these lies were bound to catch up with me but I didn't have a choice. When he came round I told him that I'd sold my phone to pay some guy off I owed money to and if he wanted to stay in touch with me he'd have to buy me a new one.

I was really pushing it but he took me out and bought me a new phone.

"Don't sell this one," he said.

Later that day, he asked me if I'd like to come to the Sunday service with him. I thought about it for a while but after all he'd done for me, I couldn't really say no, so just before he left I arranged for him to pick me up the following Sunday morning.

"I will be there this time, I promise," I said reassuring him. The rest of that week was tough. All the negative thoughts seemed to be in overdrive and as a result I drank more than usual in an attempt to drown out the voices. I was feeling extremely depressed and no matter what time I went to sleep I'd wake up feeling as exhausted as when I went to bed.

How long my body and mind could take this barrage of drugs, drink, gambling, debt, lying, stealing, binge eating, smoking, not sleeping, medication and a head spilling over with thoughts of suicide was anyone's guess. This is what I had to put up with everyday. I had no control over what I did and every day I was as desperate for more as I was for change.

Sunday morning arrived again with the same banging on the door. To Jonnie's surprise, this time, I answered.

"I can't believe I'm going to church," I said as we made our way down to his car. I was a bit nervous for some reason and asked loads of questions on the way, trying to get a picture of what to expect.

The church was the one Jonnie went to with his mum in Ibstock near Coalville. I'd never been there before. In fact, I hadn't been to church for a very long time but how bad could it be? To me it would be a load of old blue rinses praying to a God that I didn't believe in. We pulled into the car park and were greeted by some happy looking locals and regular churchgoers. A couple of them were big and burley ex-miners and were nothing like the stereotypical Christians I was expecting to see.

We went to the main door and as it opened something strange happened. If you've ever flown abroad on holiday then you will know what it's like when you land and they open the plane doors, letting in a blast of warm air like someone's pointed a hairdryer in your direction. Well that's what it was like when the church doors opened except it wasn't warm air that hit me that morning. It was the presence of something I hadn't felt in a long time, genuine kindness and love. It was quite over-whelming and felt lovely at first but after the initial blast I was filled with guilt and a deep shame knowing some of the terrible things I'd done over the past few years.

I felt black inside and was convinced that everyone could see me for who I was. All I wanted to do was hide from these people who seemed so content and full of life, a happy life, not the kind of life I had experienced. I couldn't look anybody straight in the eye and went to my seat feeling very uncomfortable. The music started and people began singing songs about Jesus as if they knew him personally. I sat quietly not opening my mouth once. I felt such a fake and thought if I sang everyone would look at me in disgust.

Then this guy from Los Angeles came out and preached on something or other, his name was Pastor Barry Thomas. I can't remember what he said but it was as if he was talking directly to me. I started to feel a bit weird as he spoke and the more he went on the stranger I felt. It was like something was bubbling up inside me and wanted to come out. At the end, when he asked if anyone wanted to know Jesus I knew that I did and wanted to put my hand up, but I was so bound by the negative thoughts in my head I kept my arms firmly by my sides, passing on the opportunity. I was kind of glad it had all finished. What I thought was going to be a stroll in the park turned into a very uncomfortable situation. I wasn't ready to confront my demons and didn't think I ever would be. All I wanted to do was get out of there. I wanted to run away from all this niceness, I wasn't used to being around it and didn't feel I deserved to be treated as if I was one of them.

On the way back Jonnie asked me what I thought about the service.

"Mmm" I said "They seemed nice, but I don't think it's my cup of tea."

I thanked him for taking me and he dropped me off at home. I thought that was the end of it but I was greatly mistaken.

That afternoon as I was making dinner my mind was all over the shop. I sat down to eat and as I was shovelling the food in my mouth, for reasons I couldn't explain I started sobbing. Now I say sobbing because it wasn't superficial and was coming from somewhere deep within me, somewhere I hadn't been before. I was feeling very strange and a bit scared; so I decided to call Jonnie to ask him what was going on.

"Hi Jonnie, it's Johnny" I said trying to keep the tears back. "I'm crying and I don't know why, what's going on? What have you done to me you weirdo?" I asked half joking.

Jonnie seemed shocked to hear me so broken on the other end of the phone but was very understanding. He told me,

"The feeling that you're getting deep inside is Jesus knocking on the door of your heart. He wants you to let him in and spend the rest of your life with him." I didn't quite understand what that meant but there was definitely something real, yet very strange going on inside me.

I was in a right state and told him I had to go, putting the phone down and feeling a little numb.

I tried to brush those feelings off over the next few days and decided I wouldn't go to the service the following week if ever again. Jonnie kept calling to encourage me but I was afraid of making a commitment to go but at the same time I didn't want to let him down, especially after all he'd done for me. I was fast approaching a crossroads in my life. On the one hand I wanted to get rid of all the baggage that was holding me down and on the other hand had no idea what would happen if I gave my life to Jesus. Doing drugs, gambling and all the other stuff was who I had become and I didn't know any other way of life. To be honest, just the thought of becoming a Christian scared the s**t out of me! I mean, I never was one to hold back on anything so if I went for it, it would have to be all or nothing. If I gave it my all would it mean I'd become all-boring and lose my identity? Or would I become some unrecognisable bloke that just disappeared off the face of the earth and never amounted to anything? I didn't know the answers and these were real concerns for me. I wanted to be set free but at what cost?

32

Firmly rooted

I felt confused; my head was a complete mess but I had decided that the next time Jonnie called I would go to the Sunday service with him. He came and picked me up the following weekend and as we went into the church, those same feelings of guilt and darkness, that I'd felt weeks before, came flooding back, bringing with them a heavy sense of conviction in my heart.

The pastor came out and spoke again but this time I felt differently towards him. I was ready to receive what he had to say. At the end, he once again gave out a call for those who didn't know Jesus.

"If there is someone that does not know Jesus and would like to enter into a life changing relationship with him today then I would like you to put your hand up. I would like everyone to close their eyes so that only I shall see. Afterwards we can say a prayer of repentance and acceptance together and you can be set free in his name."

Well, he didn't have to say any more. I knew exactly what I was going to do. Something had been eating away inside me during the whole service; and at one point I thought I was going to be sick. I had absolutely nothing to lose, I'd give God seven days to prove himself and change my life. Even though I was nervous I put my hand in the air and showed the Pastor that I wanted to change and give Jesus a chance. He acknowledged my courage; "I see your hand." After the service finished we went into a back room and said a prayer together.

That day, Sunday the 10th of October 2004 at 12.20pm, I asked God to forgive me for all the terrible things I'd done and declared that from that point, I would follow Jesus for the rest of my life and turn away from what I knew was wrong. I acknowledged that I believed Jesus to be the Son of God and accepted the free gift of his Holy Spirit right there and then! Wow! I couldn't believe it. I'd actually done it. I knew that I'd done something very special and when I left that small back room to join the others for tea and coffee, I felt strangely warm and light. A weight had been lifted, I wasn't floating six feet in the air and no wings or halo appeared but I felt, in my heart, that I was acceptable to God and had, quite possibly, made a real lasting commitment, one that had the potential to change my life for eternity.

I told anyone who would listen to me what I had done and was congratulated by other church goers. Some prayed for me and others gave me words of encouragement. When I told Jonnie he was over the moon. All of his work and belief had paid off. He had carried out what God had asked and as a result another soul had been saved. I'd just had an encounter with Jesus that was to have a lasting impact on my life and, hopefully, touch many others.

When I got home I felt so different inside. I naively thought things were going to change all by themselves and the next day, I half expected to wake up looking physically different as well. I wasn't disappointed to see the same old me in the mirror but was disappointed to find that I still had the urge to drink and gamble.

Sadly, later that day, I found myself in the bookies losing again and getting drunk whilst, at the same time, telling people in the pub I'd changed and become a Christian. They must have thought I'd totally lost the plot. Over the next two weeks I didn't attend church meetings and kept away from Christians, I felt I didn't deserve to be around such decent people while I was continuing to indulge in all the same things that had led to such misery before. In fact, I even started to question whether I'd done the right thing or not and began to slowly slip away again. My mum knew I'd become a Christian, as did the rest of my family but nobody really believed it. Some people thought it was just another angle, that I was going to con church goers for money and that my so called "new found faith" was all a big scam. To be honest, at the time, I wasn't even sure of my intentions. Getting money out of people to feed my addictions had always been on the cards. Anyway, my mum wanted it to be true and came round to see me one afternoon. I was in bed when she got there; I'd been up until about five am doing coke and talking about God to some bloke from the pub. I stumbled out of bed looking and feeling s**t, let her in then collapsed onto the sofa drinking copious amounts of water in an attempt to re-hydrate. My mum disappeared into the loo. Unbeknown to me she'd got hold of Pastor Barry's number and was on the phone to him, telling him the state I was in and saying, "If you don't want to lose him, then come round and encourage him to address his issues."

When she reappeared from the loo I'd no idea she'd been on the phone and within twenty minutes the buzzer to my flat sounded. I peered out the window and saw Barry and his wife Josephine standing by the front door. "Oh no," I whispered loudly. "Mum, Barry's here you've got to tell him I'm not here!" I told her, but before I could finish she'd picked up the intercom and buzzed them in.

"What did you do that for?" I barked at her scrambling into the bedroom to put something a bit smarter on. I was feeling crap and the last thing I wanted to do was be with people who were clearly living on a different level to me.

My mum let them in and I came out to see them.

"Hi," I said looking embarrassed about the state I was in. As always they were very understanding and invited me and mum out for lunch so they could have a chat with me. I accepted, and we went out for a carvery. We talked for ages and they explained some stuff to me, which put a lot of things into context and answered some of my questions. One thing I will always remember is something that Josephine said to me. It was approaching Christmas once again and she told me a story about the Christmas tree and the apple tree. The Christmas tree looks fantastic. People would gather around it to gaze upon its beauty, it has tinsel and decorations all over it and gifts underneath, but no matter how beautiful or big it was it had no roots and would only last for a few weeks and at the end of the festive season it would wither and die. The apple tree, on other hand, was firmly rooted in the ground and no matter what the weather; it would bear a steady stream of fruit. It would last for many years and would reproduce and, although it might not be as spectacular as the Christmas tree, it had a consistency and stability that gave it a beauty that no fake or uprooted tree could ever have. This was incredible. It meant so much to me and those words rang true in my heart and mind. These were just the words that I needed to hear to help me put things into context and to help me with the decisions I needed to make.

I realised that day I'd always been like that Christmas tree. I'd always wanted the 'WOW factor', wherever I went I always had to be the centre of attention and sadly, like the Christmas tree they were always fleeting moments of joy that would wither and die. After all, I had no roots. After our conversation I could see that if I wanted to be like the apple tree I had to be rooted deep into the ground so that I could grow stronger and have stability. I'd have to learn to be committed and consistent, sacrificing momentary glory for an eternal steadfastness. I left there that day with a renewed faith in Jesus and hoped that I could change for the better but still had no idea to what extent and when.

33
Revelation

Things happened pretty quickly after that and one afternoon I was out in the pub drinking quite heavily, sponging drinks as usual, when a guy walked in and came straight over to me.

"You know for a Christian, you aren't half drinking a lot" he said and then turned round and walked off. I'd never seen this bloke before yet when he said that my heart skipped a beat. How on earth did he know I was a Christian?" I necked my beer and walked out the pub. I had to get out of there it was all just too weird.

I made my way home; I was really spooked by what had just happened. When I got in I suddenly felt really sick, like I'd normally feel the day after a skin full of beer but it felt like I was having my hangover now, in the middle of the afternoon during a drink!

The feeling lasted about ten minutes and when it had subdued my mind was flooded with thoughts of what I had been doing. I knew it was God talking to me, telling me that he wanted my life to reflect the decision that I had made. At that precise moment my decision to follow Jesus could not be seen by others through my actions or behaviour. God wanted people to know that he had my heart, not just by what I said but, more importantly, how I lived. This was a revelation to me.

I asked God to help me change my life, from that moment, to make this a reality.

There was a lot to change and after that day I made a promise to God that with his help I would stop drinking and gambling. This was never easy. I'd tried this many times before but had always weakened or succumbed to temptation, however now that I had God on my side it was going to be different. This time I was going to succeed!

As each day passed I started to feel differently towards drink, drugs and gambling. They seemed to be losing the power they once had over me and I was beginning to sleep better as a result. Normally, I wouldn't get to sleep until the early hours of the morning but now when my head hit the pillow, I felt a peace and excitement that melted my worries and cares away, leaving me free to sleep, knowing that there was a future for me and now I had hope and a reason to live.

Days turned into weeks and I'd not drank, done drugs or gambled for a month. I couldn't believe it and nor could anyone else who knew me, it was fantastic!

Things were changing big time and I was spending all my spare time reading the bible and praying. God was staying true to his word, confirming all the things that Barry said he could and would do in my life given half a chance. I was slowly being liberated from one vice after another. I couldn't get enough of Jesus.

One morning, I went into the bathroom to take my anti depressant medication as I had done every day for the past ten years, when I heard God talking to me again. It was a small but distinct voice inside that was different to all the other stuff that usually went round in my head.

"What are you doing? The voice said. I thought about it for a second.

"I don't know what am I doing?"

Then the voice came again. "Take your tablet into the front room, put it on the table and ask it some questions."

It seemed like a really weird thing to do. I mean there I was on medication for supposedly having mental health problems and God wanted me to go into the front room and talk to my tablets. Now that was crazy! Anyway, I was intrigued as to what was going to happen so I did what I was told. I put the tablet down on the table and said, "Hi, my name's Johnny, what's your name?" The tablet, like all other tablets, said nothing. So, I asked another question. "I've been with you now for many years. Can you tell me who I really am?" Nothing. So I asked my final question, this time on a more serious note. "Can I trust you and do you love me?" The tablet remained silent but inside I heard the same voice again, this time louder and more direct than before. "For years you thought your identity was sickness and addiction and have put your trust in a piddely little tablet that can't even answer your questions. Go and throw them away and put your trust in the living God!" At that moment everything made complete sense to me and I decided I was going to put my trust in God. I knew it wasn't going to be easy but I believed I could be healed by God through faith and at that moment be accepted and receive the healing that God was offering me. Sure, I was going to have some sickness as a result of withdrawing from medication but I knew that if I turned to God for comfort and strength during the hard times he would see me through. It was time for me to turn away from being a victim, and through my relationship with Jesus Christ, become a victor. No longer would darkness have a hold on me!

The next day I decided to go to the doctor's and tell him that I was cured and no longer needed to be on income support, as I wasn't sick anymore. You should have seen his face; he couldn't believe what I was saying and commented on how different I looked. I told him that I'd met a man named Jesus who had known me for a long time and had shown me how to become the person I should have always been, and how by believing in him I'd been set free from all the burdens I'd carried for years. He was gob smacked and after he signed me off the sick, I left, never to return.

A few days later I was in the kitchen of my flat making tea. I was having a chicken korma and rice and as I was taking it out of the microwave my sleeve caught the door and my plate went smashing on the floor, leaving yellow food stains and chicken everywhere. I shouted, "For crying out loud!" As I heard my self say those words I realised that God had changed me in such a way, that even in a crisis or under pressure, nothing bad came out my mouth. Normally I would have sworn like a trooper. I couldn't believe it and fell to the floor laughing my head off and singing hymns. At least I had got enough food to spill! By now, I'd stopped swearing, drinking, doing drugs and gambling, it felt awesome. Everyday, as I grew to know and trust God, my life became better and better.

Later that month I was getting baptised and was so excited about it. I still had a tag on my ankle and had to reassure some of the older folk at the church I wouldn't get electrocuted as I went in the water. Earlier that week I had been sent a letter from the courts calling me in for a hearing as before I'd committed myself to Jesus, I'd gone over my curfew by twenty-nine hours. So there was a real possibility I could be going back to prison.

My baptismal day came round and the church building was packed. There were thirteen of us getting dipped that Morning, including Jonnie's Mum, Dad and sister (Dianne, Dave and Lisa Cave.) We were all getting baptised by Jonnie and Pastor Barry. The day went wonderfully well. People gave individual testimonies about how their lives had changed. When I came out of the water, I threw my arms in the air in celebration and knew in my heart that my past was firmly behind me. I even stopped smoking a few days later and the only immediate obstacle I had left to face was the Judge in court.

The next Monday, my Mum and Barry escorted me to court. Barry was there to give me support and to speak on my behalf if necessary. Things were totally different than when I'd been sent down before. I was no longer afraid of going to prison because I felt free on the inside and had prepared myself for the worst. I would simply pray for a good outcome and just face the music. When I was called in I was asked by the Judge why I had gone over my curfew. I don't think they were prepared for my answer. I said "To be honest your honour, I have no excuse whatsoever. I had no regard for authority and didn't care what happened to me and for that I ask your forgiveness. However a few weeks ago I became a Christian and have spent that time addressing many issues in my life with the help of my Pastor and family and have made a clean start." I went on to explain that I was throwing myself on the mercy of the court but was prepared to go to prison if that's what the Judges felt was necessary. The Judges seemed flustered and went out to deliberate. They seemed to be gone for ages and when they came back in, I took a deep breath, expecting the worse. "Mr Kinch," said the Judge. "We take it very seriously when someone breaks their curfew order. In your case, twenty-nine hours is completely unacceptable."

Oh dear, this didn't sound good.

"However, you have escaped a custodial sentence this time and we are going to give you one more chance. You will be serving a community service order of 180 hours over a six month period, and let me tell you this, we will certainly not be as lenient if we see you again! You may go."

I looked round at Barry and my Mum and all three of us had beaming smiles. I was over the moon. "Thank you God," I whispered. They made an appointment for me to go to probation that week so that they could find a place where I could do my community service.

I believe 100% that God's hand was orchestrating the proceedings that day. Later that week, when I went to probation, they realised that there weren't any spaces left with the usual painting gangs, so they had to rummage around to find me a placement. The only one that was available was working in a church canteen at the other end of town. To me this was the confirmation I needed. God *was* looking after me. Over the next six months I buckled down, completing my hours without a problem and steadily became healthier due to my new lifestyle.

I almost couldn't believe it, but it was true, my life had changed beyond recognition. The person I once was, was now dead and buried and I had found a life in Christ that can only be described as awesome! And as if that's not enough, not only had God set me free from the painful, life sucking burdens I was carrying, but he also showed me that through him anything was possible! I can clearly remember during my lowest points in life, how thoughts of suicide were quite literally trying to take me out. It was as if someone was trying to rob me of the life I had been given. The bible says in John 10:10;

"The thief comes only to steal and kill and destroy."

I know for a fact that the thief (satan) was trying to steal my life before I got a chance to find it in Christ, and if you have read all of this book, then you will be in no doubt that he was also trying (through the power of negative suggestion) to destroy me. My mind was a battleground, one where satan was wining, but thankfully God was there when I needed him most and after taking a chance on Christ and through the power of his spirit and word, I was no longer a slave to the thoughts that had held me down for so long, but was set free inwardly by the renewing of my mind.

Romans 12:2;

"Do not conform yourselves to the standards of this world, but let God transform you inwardly by a complete change of your mind. Then you will be able to know the will of God – what is good and is pleasing to him and is perfect."

It was as if God had his hand in my head and was turning the cogs back the other way. It was so real I could actually feel movement in my mind. When certain situations arose that would have made me act a certain way before, now due to the renewing of my mind I felt and thought differently. God had given me the power to change my thoughts and subsequently my actions!

34

A new beginning

The story doesn't end here, for me, it's just beginning but I've really got to wind it down otherwise it might never finish. So many things have happened to me since I became a Christian that I could write another book just about the first six months.

When God gives you life he gives it in abundance!

Anyway, not long after I finished my community service I went off to study theology at Covenant College in Coventry. On the first day there I met my wife, Anneka. We got engaged six weeks later and married in July 2006.

I've been a Christian now for three years and have never once gone back to my old ways. Thank God. Since leaving college I've been back in a hostel but this time as a support worker, where my past experiences have helped me to bring many others through tough times in their lives. Some have also become Christians along the way, breaking free from the same chains that held me back for so many years.

It's great to be alive and I thank God every day for what he's done for me. Giving my life to Jesus was and is the best decision that I ever made. I have experienced so many things, on so many levels in life. I have chased down what I thought were my dreams, even at the expense of myself and others. I have done just about everything to fill the void inside but found no real lasting joy. Then on the day I gave myself to God and made knowing him my goal, the emptiness inside me was finally filled. Not with something temporal like before, but with an eternal God who loves me and will never let me down. Like I have so many others in the past. Living life knowing God and not just merely existing without him, is the most amazing and rewarding experience that any human being could ever have. My *soul* purpose in life is to know God and because he set me free from the inner prison I was in, I find it a pure joy to tell others about the amazing free gift of eternal life through Jesus Christ that is waiting for them if they will only believe. That is why I have written this book. I once was lost but now I'm found, I once was blind but now I see, I once was skint but now I'm prosperous! I once was empty but now I'm full to over flowing. This is the very nature of God himself. He is a restorer of broken lives and hearts and God has brought restoration to every aspect of my life. I hope that by reading my story, you too might come to see that Jesus loves you, and is waiting to change your life in the same monumental way that he has done for me and millions like me! For me, becoming a Christian and following Jesus was just the beginning of the greatest part of my life. This is how C. S. Lewis puts it; at the end of the Chronicles of Narnia…

"For us, this is the end of all the stories … but for them it was only the beginning of the real story. All their life in this world…had only been the cover and title page: now at last they were beginning chapter one of the great story, which no one on earth has read, which goes on for ever and in which every chapter is better than the one before."

No matter what obstacles are in your life, no matter how bad things have become, there is a way out and the way is Jesus! Believe me I know!

"I am the way, the truth and the life…." John 14 v 6.

If you want to know more about how your life could change like mine please email me at:
doyouneedamiracle@gmail.com

Or alternatively visit my website at:
www.doyouneedamiracle.co.uk

I would love to hear from you!
May God bless you.

Johnny Kinch